GW00859281

Adam Ate with Dinosaurs

*The theory of evolution, how it came into prominence,
why it continues to influence our thinking
and what the Bible teaches about origins*

Adam Ate with Dinosaurs

Christopher J Tokeley

ATHENA PRESS
LONDON

ISBN 978 1 84748 708 7

First published 2010 by
ATHENA PRESS
Queen's House, 2 Holly Road
Twickenham TW1 4EG
United Kingdom

Scripture verses, unless otherwise indicated, are taken from the
Holy Bible, *New International Version* © 1973, 1978, 1984 by the
International Bible Society and used with permission.
Excerpts by Ronald Clark from *The Survival of Charles Darwin* (©
Ronald Clark, 1985) are reproduced by permission of PFD
(www.pfd.co.uk) on behalf of the estate of Ronald Clark.
Every effort has been made to trace the copyright holders
of works quoted within this book and obtain permission.
The publisher apologises for any omission and is happy to make
necessary changes in subsequent print runs.

Printed for Athena Press

Dedicated to
the late Rev. Chandos C H M Morgan C B, M A, R N,
one-time Archdeacon of the Royal Navy
and Rector, St Margaret Lothbury, City of London

Acknowledgements

I would like to thank my nephew, David, for checking the early manuscript, Anthony Stevens for his encouragement and advice, without which I might have given up before the book had been completed, my wife, Brenda, who must have checked my English grammar many times, and our daughter Judy for her secretarial skills.

A Message from the Author

Usually publishers call this the preface, but I want it to be much more personal. This book is about creation and the world in which we live. My overwhelming desire for those who read this book is that they have information about the creation versus evolution debate. Evolution is the unproven theory that all forms of life originated by descent from earlier forms.

Macroevolution is the unproven theory that one species can change over billions of years into another distinct species: man evolving from fish, as often casually referred to in nature documentaries on television as if it is fact. This teaching the author rejects.

Microevolution takes place when genetic information produces variation within species. The effects of microevolution that we see every day in the huge variety in the feline species provide just one example.

Everyone knows about evolution, as it is taught throughout our education system, through the media, and in our libraries and museums. Furthermore, theistic evolution is taught in most of our churches. For most people, an alternative explanation for life on this planet does not exist. Unknown to most people there are books, tapes, videos and organisations that teach that special creation took place a few thousand years ago and was the work of God, who is the author of a book we call the Bible. The Bible has been described as a love letter from God. Many of the authors of the books and websites listed in this publication are scientists who believe that our planet is a young Earth that was created as explained in the first chapters of the Bible. Some are leaders in their particular scientific disciplines.

This book is a resource book: if it does not provide the answers to your questions it will point you to other authors who can help you and give a more detailed account. If your appetite has been whetted for more reading material on creation issues, there is a select bibliography of works written by scientists who believe in the Bible's account of creation. There is also a list of publications, contacts and websites that do not adhere to evolutionary ideas but instead state the belief that the Bible is the book that tells us the truth about life and how it started on our planet. I have found that many people want help as to how they may be assured that what the Bible teaches is correct, and a better focus on how it conflicts with what we are taught by the media about how life began, dinosaurs, the age of the Earth, etc. Why are there natural disasters when the Church teaches that God is a loving person? People often ask how they can believe the Bible when scientific opinion is not in harmony with it. In fact, what we hear from the media puts science and the Bible into direct conflict. If the Bible is the authoritative Word of God, then true scientific investigation can never conflict with its teaching on creation and the origins of life. It is not necessary to disregard the first eleven chapters of the Book of Genesis to bring the Bible into harmony with science, as many pastors and teachers do today. The reader will have to interpret scientific evidence differently and with an open mind, not one that has been blinded by decades of teaching of atheistic evolutionary ideas and principles based on unproven theories.

This book has been written by someone who searched for the truth about where we originated, who learnt science at school and found that what was taught never gripped the imagination. Statistics show that not a lot has changed in sixty years, as few sixth-form students opt for science subjects today and universities are closing courses.

Even as a child I was interested in the world about me and in the latest scientific advancements. My particular hobby was making exact scale models from a book on aircraft. By good fortune my neighbour owned a wood-turning factory and he had a ready supply of various shapes, many of which only needed sanding and sawing to become part of an aircraft. It fascinated me that we continued to build large aircraft needing ever-longer runways to take off when the obvious answer to this problem was vertical-take-off aircraft carrying several hundred passengers. For an essay on this subject as a teenager, I won a runner-up prize in a national daily newspaper: a day out to an international air show to meet the test pilots! A young aircraft designer's dream come true.

I never imagined that years later I would live in the centre of UK aviation industry and make friends with those engaged in the development of Concorde and navigational inventions.

After thirty years in the City of London, I left a career in international trade finance, which included finance for the purchase of aircraft. I crossed into a very different occupation where scientists of many disciplines were all around me. This gave me the opportunity to learn more about many of the scientific events that hit the headlines. I have a very high regard for the openness of many scientists and their desire to seek answers to the most perplexing problems that we face today, whether they be modern farming practices or the mystery of DNA.

What amazes and disturbs me most are people who claim to be disciples of Christ and yet refuse to believe that the first chapters of the Book of Genesis present a factual account of what happened. I have often asked the same people if they have ever read a book whose author believes that the first eleven chapters of the first book of the Bible are fact. The answer is always a hesitant no! One minister of a church was shocked to learn that I believed in special creation, that Adam was a real man and that the flood account was factual, reporting a worldwide event. I mentioned that Jesus and the Apostles taught all these and that there was ample evidence that they believed these accounts were factual. He never quoted the Bible to me but said he relied on the word of a scientist friend. Who are we to trust: the Bible, the authoritative Word of God, or a scientist? I have no animosity towards Christians who do not share my views. The love of our Lord Jesus Christ, shown in His death and resurrection, is the grace that bonds us together.

I readily acknowledge the enormous contribution that scientific research has made into the development of technologies that we take for granted in this age of fast cars, fast food and mobile phones. We live and see dramatic changes almost daily, and sometimes wonder when the pace will slow! It is a disappointment to me that so few decide to study science.

It is amazing to experience the power and reliability of the jet engine. With our belts fastened we are propelled to a height of thousands of metres in minutes. So too am I held in wonder by the progress of modern medicine as failing parts of our bodies are repaired. The relentless research into the causes and cure of our biggest killer, cancer, never fails to bring encouragement to all who take an interest in medicine. This tireless quest brings new treatment and the hope, perhaps, of a vaccine for some types. So this book is not written in order to bash scientists or even ministers of religion, or even question the worth of scientific progress, but the reader may want to look again at what the Bible says and then again at the interpretation of scientific evidence. What I have found in my research for this book may shock you.

Scientists are quoted in this book who are qualified to give their interpretation of scientific evidence that surrounds the mystery of when Earth was created and how human life came to be; their account corroborates the teaching of the oldest book in the world, the Bible. So the information drawn comes from many scientists and many Bible teachers and, of course, the Bible itself. To be fair to those who may object to this book, I have even quoted scientists who hold evolutionary views.

Part One of this book is very disturbing. No one likes to learn that they have been deceived. If we are honest we can remember at least one occasion when someone managed to deceive us. I'll own up to the fact I was deceived at a car boot sale. I usually enjoy car boot sales. At one car boot sale a man looked through my CDs and offered twenty pounds for six, waving a large note. As I had only just set up my stall and could not give change for his large banknote, the man waved to a distant stall and said it was his, and told me he would be back with the correct amount. He was never seen again, and nor were my CDs. Hey! If you want to pay for the CDs now, send the money to my publisher! The trouble is we do not know when we are being deceived. If we knew, then there of course would be no deception. To find we've been deceived is perhaps the rudest awakening ever, and most people are deeply upset. People fall prey to scams every day. Many prefer not to explore this area in life and are content to believe the impossible. Many people are embarrassed and would not own up to being duped.

Bibles were burnt at St Paul's Cross, London, at the command of Cuthbert Tunstall, Bishop of London, during November 1526, and other books have undergone a similar fate when the order of the day has been challenged. I hope this book will challenge us on how we have received and adopted the theory of evolution into our thinking and thought processes. Evolutionary teaching has been taken on board by generations, so we no longer read or study the Bible's account of creation and certainly don't believe that dinosaurs could have been around at the time of Adam, even if he really existed. Our generation has been conned into believing we have evolved from apes and therefore we no longer seek alternative views. The majority of people who occupy pews in our churches will not take kindly to this book. If it makes us think about what the Bible teaches about the world in which we live and how it came into being, then it will have achieved its aim. If we wipe the dust off possibly the first eleven chapters of the Bible, it will have achieved its objective of making us delve deeper into the great spiritual truths. We shall then begin to realise that the Bible is correct about every detail and scientific matter upon which it touches. If this book improves our relationship with the living God, it will have served a divine purpose far beyond the power of any human author. Only the Holy Spirit can take paper, glue and ink and make them into something that lives and moves our deepest thoughts and motivates our very being.

I believe that we live in a time of unprecedented deception. I have seen through the deception of the theory of evolution as it is paraded today by the media. I had a rather rude awakening. Today the media seems to be the enemy of science as much as it is of the Gospel. But the power of God is greater than that of the media. I will end this introduction by suggesting you will need a Bible; so if you don't have one, buy one with this book or ask your granny for the family Bible.

This book is in three parts, so that when you buy it you get three for the price of one. The first part shows how we have been deceived. Yes, I know history is a bore, but sometimes we cannot understand how we have been influenced in our thinking today without knowing how famous people of the past still control our thought processes.

Every time we switch on the electric light we are indebted to Michael Faraday, a true Christian. Charles Darwin perhaps holds more sway over our thinking than anyone else in recent history. Having studied the life of Charles Darwin I have come to have a great affection for him and, even though we do not always share the same views, he would have been my friend. He needed a close friend who was a true believer in Jesus Christ and who had the patience and courage to stay by his side when his favourite daughter, Annie, died and he was grief-stricken. I believe that his theory has held back the progress of scientific discovery on many occasions because of inbred preconceptions that conflict with true science. It is not altogether Darwin's fault that men close their minds to other interpretations of scientific evidence.

The second part is about the Bible. It is remarkable how God gave His message of salvation to us. Chuck Missler has described the Bible as a message from the edge of eternity. Few Christians seem to be aware of the facts about its origin. When challenged about the authenticity of the Bible they have no answer. It is the most criticised book on our airwaves, but nevertheless we can rely on its authenticity, its reliability and its infallibility.

The third part of this book looks at some aspects of science. I hope this will spur you on to read books by scientists who believe that the entire Bible is God-breathed and means exactly what it says and does not conflict with true science.

At the end of each part, under the title 'Weekend Reading', I have nominated one book taken from the select bibliography that complements what I have written. Each book will take the average reader about four hours to read. The book could be slipped into your hand luggage to be read on the flight to your favourite holiday resort – or, more likely, during the voting at the Euro-vision Song Contest!

The first annex to this book is probably the most helpful part, because few know of the existence of the organisations listed, which can supply books that are not on sale in your local Christian bookshop. There is no sinister reason why these books are not on their shelves. The scientist authors of the books are highly qualified in their disciplines, most at PhD level. Most of our Christian bookshops only sell books by popular authors.

Except for one or two, this seems to exclude scientists. Perhaps this is because science is not a popular subject. They only sell a very small proportion of the total of Christian books published each year. Christian bookshops are strapped for cash and cannot keep in stock books they are not sure will clear from their shelves quickly. I hope this book will encourage you to study the Bible using the material provided by organisations mentioned in this annex. If you are not acquainted with the world's best-selling publication, and are mystified as to references like Job, Timothy and 2 Corinthians, etc., then there is an annex giving the names of the books of the Bible. Finally, there is a select bibliography. Many of the books mentioned can be ordered through your local bookshop, which I hope you support. Some may be out of print, but then there are libraries and second-hand shops where they may be found. There is also the internet. Your public library will usually, for a small fee, try to obtain any book you request, and they also hold books in their archives.

Quotable Quotes are in the main taken from some of my favourite authors and I have tried to put them before the chapters on the subjects to which they refer.

Christopher J Tokeley

Contents

Part One

Quotable Quotes

It is a comforting thought, for man in himself does not possess knowledge. Man gropes about as though walking in darkness. His way is beset on all sides with problems that press in upon him and clamour for a solution. To these problems man can often turn but an uncomprehending glance, for he has no knowledge to apply to their solution. Professing to know and also to be wise, nevertheless he does not know, and hence his decisions and judgements are not those of wisdom and knowledge. With God, however, knowledge is to be found, as well as the ability to apply this knowledge. God is all-knowing and God is all-wise. To be able to address such a God is a blessing indeed. Happy are those who can say THOU to a God of knowledge; they possess a treasure that cannot be matched upon the earth where darkness and ignorance reign.

E J Young, *The Way Everlasting,* Edinburgh, The Banner of Truth Trust, pp.20–21 (commenting on verse 2 of Psalm 139)

...therefore, since through God's mercy we have this ministry, we do not lose heart. Rather, we have renounced secret and shameful ways; we do not use deception, nor do we distort the Word of God. On the contrary, by setting forth the truth plainly we commend ourselves to every man's conscience in the sight of God. And even if our gospel is veiled, it is veiled to those who are perishing. The god of this age has blinded the minds of unbelievers, so that they cannot see the light of the gospel of the glory of Christ, who is the image of God. For we do not preach ourselves, but Jesus Christ as Lord, and ourselves as your servants for Jesus' sake. For God, who said, 'Let light shine out of darkness', made his light shine in our hearts to give us the light of the knowledge of the glory of God in the face of Christ.

2 Corinthians 4:1–6

Submit yourselves for the Lord's sake to every authority instituted among men: whether to the king, as the supreme authority, or to governors, who are sent by him to punish those who do wrong and to commend those who do right. For it is God's will that by doing good you should silence the ignorant talk of foolish men. Live as free men, but do not use your freedom as a cover-up for evil; live as servants of God. Show proper respect to everyone; Love the brotherhood of believers, fear God, honour the king.

1 Peter 2:13–17

I

Understanding the Influence that Darwin has over our Thinking

> There is a way that seems right to a man but in the end it leads to death.
>
> Proverbs 14:12

We need to understand that the theory of evolution has permeated our thinking and how this has influenced our views – for the Christian in particular, our views on the first eleven chapters of Genesis and moral issues. This theory challenges the Bible's claim to be the infallible Word of God. Because the Church has taken it on board it has led to the withdrawal of God's blessing on the Church in the West. A good friend of mine believes that God is angry at the Church because it has ceased to believe in the inerrancy of His Word.

We need to ask ourselves some important questions. Do we believe everything that is taught in our education system and by the media about evolution? Are we prepared to question what we are told? Is the Earth billions of years old, and did man evolve from ape men after dinosaurs became extinct, and did our ancestors crawl out of the sea? These are the ideas that we are bombarded with by atheistic thinkers. However, there are other views we seldom hear which we should seriously consider. Can we counter from Scripture the atheistic evolutionary teaching our children or grandchildren receive in school, through books and over the airwaves? We may be worried about what they read in their leisure time or watch on television. We are worried there are books with storylines about witchcraft or magic, but are we aware of the influence of evolutionary teaching in the classroom that will undo the good work of many Christian parents and turn them away from God? Perhaps our children are turning to books on wizardry and magic because we have succeeded in taking the supernatural out of the Bible! Have we read any books recently claiming to offer an alternative view to the theory of evolution?

A survey I conducted showed only about 5% of churchgoing people read books about creation and the pre-Abrahamic period. The most popular books were on prayer, the Christian life, missionary work and the study of the New Testament. I hope to encourage you to read books, watch videos and listen to audio tapes that give biblical teaching. This is teaching that does not conflict with scientific evidence and yet honours the teaching of the Bible, and which gives God all the glory for the wonders of the universe in which we live.

I hope this book will help answer important questions. Who were Adam and Eve? Who wrote the first chapters of Genesis and when? Where do dinosaurs fit into ancient history, and are they mentioned in the Bible? How old is the Earth and man? Why do some translations of the Bible add marginal notes that have no textual or scientific basis? Why does the Independent Television Commission (ITC) allow nudity, sexual acts and violence to be programmed? What controls their decisions and why are TV programmes likely to deteriorate even further? I hope the answers to these questions will be easy to understand. They will surprise you, but you may be alarmed to find how an atheistic 'theory' has permeated our thinking. The answers will be short, only because there is a limitation of space in any book for readers with no time to waste. I remember when I commuted for thirty-five minutes to town each day seeing a fellow commuter reading Tolstoy's *War and Peace*; I wonder if he has finished reading it a decade or so later. However, a select bibliography is given at the end of this book. I hope you will read these books and the passages of Scripture to which I refer and go on to study for yourself when you have finished reading this book.

Does it matter what we believe about the origin of the cosmos?

I believe it matters. Let me explain. I know several folk who have built kit cars and they drive them. I wish I had their engineering skills. These friends told me how they constructed their cars and the time it took them. How would they feel if I doubted their word? Sometimes people are very critical and envious when they see something they know they were incapable of creating, whether it is a kit car or a flower arrangement. Sometimes they belittle the work or take the credit themselves. So it is with the theory of evolution; it takes away from God the credit due to Him. We can anger God, we can grieve the Holy Spirit and rob our Lord Jesus Christ of the glory due to Him, through what we have taken on board from atheistic teaching. It will also put doubts in our minds about our faith and retard our relationship with our Lord Jesus Christ.

> For by him all things were created: things in heaven and on earth, visible and invisible, whether thrones or powers or rulers or authorities; all things were created by him and for him.
>
> Colossians 1:16

What we believe must give Jesus Christ *all* the glory, praise and honour. The theory of evolution does not do that, even when applied in a theistic context. Later I will explain how we can trust what the Bible says about creation. The Bible claims to be the inspired Word of God. It is also historically accurate and scientifically correct. Nicky Gumbel, who founded the popular Alpha Course, states in his book *Searching Issues*, 'Science and Christian faith are not incompatible'.[1] I hasten to add that we don't have to change one God-breathed word of the Bible or tear out the first eleven chapters of Genesis to make the Bible and science compatible.

Before answering questions about the origins of the Earth and its inhabitants, we must first look at the disturbing background to the controversy over the theory of evolution, and how it has turned people away from God and threatens to destroy the

Church in the Western world. If we do not retrace our steps to see how the theory of evolution was thrust on to the world stage of human thought, then we shall not understand the enormous problem the Church faces today in winning the minds of men and women. Many people think that our high standard of living and materialism are the causes of low church attendance and the rejection of the Gospel. However, this view must be challenged by the tremendous growth of the Church in the Americas and South-East Asia, which have similar standards of living to ours in Europe, where the Church is in serious decline.

The hidden agenda to break the Church

The year 1859 will go down in history for the birth of two mighty movements. A powerful Holy Spirit revival of the Christian Church began in New York and quickly spread to the whole of the English-speaking world and Europe. 'The second evangelical awakening', as this movement became known, witnessed a tide of blessing which swept hundreds of thousands of people into the Church. The power of the Gospel had been unleashed! The Church became a mighty missionary force, breaking new ground in China, Asia, Africa and South America. The previous three centuries had also witnessed powerful movements: the Reformation, the Puritan Fathers and the Evangelical Awakening under George Whitefield, Daniel Rowland, Howell Harris, John Cennick and John and Charles Wesley. Why has God not repeated this again on such a scale in the West since the nineteenth century? I hope you will read about these great revivals in the Church.

The other movement that would challenge the Church in Britain was heralded by the publication of Darwin's *Origin of Species by Means of Natural Selection or the Preservation of Favoured Races in the Struggle for Life* – commonly shortened to *Origin of Species* or *Origin*. Charles Darwin was not the first person to think about evolution and how man might have evolved from another species. Charles had these ideas passed down to him from his atheist father and grandfather. Darwin, when a student studying medicine at Edinburgh, was influenced by Robert Edmund

Grant, a free thinker who had based his views on those of Jean-Baptiste Lamarck and Étienne Geoffroy St-Hilaire, who believed the origin and evolution of all life was due to physical and chemical forces. These men were eventually to capture Darwin's mind. They set Darwin on his lifetime study of rocks and living creatures, which became his consuming passion.

Darwin, who completed no formal training in the sciences, was later to set forth the concept that biological life came from simpler forms by a process later called by Herbert Spencer 'the survival of the fittest'. According to Darwin's theory, man had reached his present state by a process of natural selection. Darwin was not happy with his book *Origin*, and he confided to a friend, 'You will be greatly disappointed [by the forthcoming book]; it will be grievously too hypothetical. It will very likely be of no other service than collating some facts; though I myself think I see my way approximately on the origin of the species. But, alas, how frequent, how almost universal it is in an author to persuade himself of the truth of his own dogmas.'[2]

Earlier Charles Darwin accepted the invitation to join the voyage of the *Beagle* to map the coast of South America and to be the expedition's botanist. Darwin was recommended to the Admiralty by a friend, Professor John Stevens Henslow. It was Darwin's intention to seek ordination in the Church of England, but his study of species was his compelling ambition. The voyage was to change Darwin's direction completely. Charles Darwin's spiritual education, apart from his school days in Shrewsbury, was confined to visits with his mother and sisters to the Unitarian Chapel. Susannah, Darwin's mother, was the daughter of wealthy industrialist Josiah Wedgwood, whose family were Unitarians. Unitarians deny the divinity of Jesus Christ and do not believe life is specially created.

By what appeared to be happy chance, Darwin was invited on a voyage that was to change the course of his life. Robert Fitzroy, master of the *Beagle*, wrote his account of how Darwin became part of the expedition.

> Anxious that no opportunity of collecting useful information, during the voyage, should be lost, I proposed to the Hydrographer that some well-educated and scientific person

should be sought for who would willingly share such accommodations as I had to offer, in order to profit by opportunity of visiting distant countries yet little known. Captain Beaufort approved of the suggestion, and wrote to Professor Peacock, of Cambridge, who consulted with a friend, Professor Henslow, and he named Mr Charles Darwin, grandson of Dr Darwin the poet, as a young man of promising ability, extremely fond of geology and indeed all branches of natural history. In consequence an offer was made to Mr Darwin to be my guest on board, which he accepted conditionally; permission was obtained for his embarkation, and an order given by the Admiralty that he should be borne on the ship's books for provisions. The conditions asked by Mr Darwin were, that he should be at liberty to leave the *Beagle* and retire from the expedition when he thought proper, and that he should pay a fair share of the expenses of my table.[3]

The invitation came at a difficult time for Darwin, as he had upset his father over his intention to seek ordination in the Church of England, and it was only the persuasion of Josiah Wedgwood, the doctor's father-in-law, that caused him to relent.

Darwin's record of his voyage showed that the study of botany was to fill his time and direct his motivation.

I worked to the utmost during the voyage from the mere pleasure of investigation, and from my strong desire to add a few facts to the great mass of facts in natural science. But I was also ambitious to take a fair place among scientific men, – whether more ambitious or less so than most of my fellow-workers I can form no opinion.[4]

The five-year voyage on the *Beagle* was not altogether a happy experience for either Fitzroy or Darwin. Robert Fitzroy, commander and surveyor, was an evangelical who believed the biblical account of creation. Often their views would bring them into conflict. Although they were good friends their relationship became strained after the publication of *Origin*. Fitzroy was promoted to Admiral and later became the first Meteorological Statist under the Board of Trade, the forerunner of the Meteorological Office. He developed maritime systems that have saved many lives at sea.

Darwin soon found on the voyage that he was no seaman, and illness plagued him. Several of the crew, including the ship's doctor, died. Reading his experiences one begins to develop a great affection for the young, inexperienced Darwin, as he continues his searches for fossils and living creatures on the mainland of South America while the *Beagle*'s crew are mapping the coast. Darwin is confronted by revolutions, earthquakes and the dangers of unexplored territories, and a commander who halfway through the voyage finds he has overstretched himself and tenders his resignation to the Admiralty (but fortunately for Darwin retracts his decision before the document is despatched).

The support from the Darwin family was in the form of a series of letters from relations telling of the troubles befalling Fanny, whom Charles loved dearly. Fanny Owen had been jilted at the altar by another suitor and had later married a politician. The marriage was a disaster, and this gave Charles much grief on the voyage. He collected and prepared animal and mineral specimens and despatched them back to England with his diary.

On 29 December 1839 Charles Darwin married his cousin, Emma, daughter of Josiah Wedgwood II, and set up home at 12 Upper Gower Street, London. As their family grew they moved to Downe in Kent. Sunday was as any other day for Charles, but Emma gathered the family and staff together for prayers. The children were taught a short Unitarian creed written by their grandfather: 'Jesus Christ was a person whom God sent to teach men their duty and to persuade and encourage them to practise it.'[5] Although she found it disagreeable, Emma took the children to worship at the parish church, where they were baptised and confirmed in the Church of England. Several of the household attended the evangelical Downe Chapel, which in 1851 was reformed on strict Baptist principles. At Downe, Darwin was able to give over his time, without interruption from guests, to his study and writing.

With the publication of *Origin*, leading atheistic thinkers of the day could hardly believe their luck! Someone who had been encouraged to seek ordination in the Church of England had given them ammunition with which to attack the Bible and cause even evangelical Christian theologians to doubt that the creation account of the Book of Genesis was historical.

Sometimes the course of history has been changed by what appear to be quite insignificant events. The editor of *The Times* newspaper responsible for the literary review was not interested in reviewing *Origin*, so he gave this task to an assistant. In the hands of Thomas Huxley, a convinced atheist, Darwin's book was to be a tool that would change the thinking of scientists and clergy. Huxley knew the Bible as well as many ministers. I once heard that a leading evangelical admitted that Huxley would be welcome in his pulpit because of his knowledge of the Bible! Huxley considered that the Old Testament was foundational to the doctrines of the Church. He knew that the influence of Christianity would wane if doubt could be cast on the early chapters of the Bible. If Genesis were to be doubted then who would believe what the Apostles wrote? The foundational teaching on six twenty-four-hour day creation, Adam and Eve as real people, Noah's flood as having encompassed the whole world, the fall of man and the nature of sin was under unceasing attack by Huxley, Spencer and other atheists. They found Darwin's book *Origin* the ammunition that they would use to explode the 'myth about God'.

Worse to come

Darwin turned his attention to the origin of the 'races', as he called the world's different ethnic groups. He researched the development of mammals from their conception through birth and development to maturity. He was intrigued by the similarity of the anatomy of all mammals, including man.

> His body is constructed on the same homological plan as that of other mammals. He passes through the same phases of embryo-logical development. He retains many rudimentary and useless structures, which no doubt were once serviceable. Characters occasionally make their re-appearance in him, which we have reason to believe were possessed by his early progenitors. If the origin of man had been wholly different from that of all other animals, these various appearances would be mere empty deceptions, but such an admission is incredible.[6]

The 'useless structures' are a reference to vestigial body organs such as the appendix which we have found in recent years to still have important functions.

Building on the popularity of his *Origin*, Darwin now considered he had enough material for a further book that would confirm his earlier theories. *The Descent of Man, and Selection in Relation to Sex* was published on 24 February 1871. Darwin now considered that all mammals came from the same origin, and certainly there was no room for a separate origin of man. He could no longer agree with Hooker that man was a separate species. Darwin in *The Descent of Man* takes his stand.

> The great principle of evolution stands up clear and firm, when these groups of facts are considered in connection with others, such as the mutual affinities of the members of the same group, their geographical distribution in past and present times and their geological succession. It is incredible that all these facts should speak falsely. He who is not content to look, like a savage, at the phenomena of nature as disconnected, cannot any longer believe that man is the work of a separate act of creation.[7]

> Thus we can understand how it has come to pass that man and all other vertebrate animals have been constructed on the same general model, why they pass through the same early stages of development, and why they retain certain rudiments in common. Consequently we ought frankly to admit their community of descent; to take any other view, is to admit that our own structure, and that of all animals around us, is a mere snare laid to entrap our judgement. This conclusion is greatly strengthened, if we look to the members of the whole animal series, and consider the evidence derived from their affinities or classification, their geographical distribution and geological succession. It is only our natural prejudice, and that arrogance which made our forefathers declare that they were descended from demi-gods, which leads us to demur to this conclusion. But time will before long come, when it will be thought wonderful that naturalists, who were well acquainted with comparative structure and development of man, and other mammals, should have believed that each was the work of a separate act of creation.[8]

Charles H Spurgeon, the great Baptist preacher, wrote in February 1887 concerning Darwin's theories, 'I have read a good deal on the subject, and have never yet seen a fact, or the tail of a fact, which indicated the rise of one species of animal to another. The theory has been laid down, and facts fished up to support it. I believe it to be a monstrous error in philosophy, which will be a theme for ridicule before another twenty years.'[9] Unfortunately, Spurgeon was too optimistic.

Darwin also believed that man had no natural or God-given inclination to believe in a creator, but that man's worship of a God was due not to instinct but what was handed down from generation to generation in a civilised society.

> There is no evidence that man was aboriginally endowed with ennobling belief in the existence of an Omnipotent God. On the contrary there is ample evidence, derived not from hasty travellers, but from men who have long resided with savages, that numerous races have existed, and still exist, who have no idea of one or more gods, and who have no words in their languages to express such an idea.[10]

Darwin went further than to believe that man was descended from the same origins as other mammals but that different 'races' were superior to others. He believed that Caucasians were superior to Negroes and Australian Aborigines. In his *Descent of Man* he makes it clear that he believes that what he calls 'civilised races' will replace 'savage races'.

> At some future period, not very distant as measured by centuries, the civilised races of man will almost certainly exterminate, and replace, the savage races throughout the world. At the same time the anthropomorphous apes, as Professor Schaaffhausen has remarked, will no doubt be exterminated. The break between man and his nearest allies will then be wider, for it will intervene between man in a more civilised state, as we may hope, even than the Caucasian, and some ape as low as a baboon, instead of as now between the negro or Australian and the gorilla.[11]

Darwin is saying that Negroes and Aborigines had not evolved as far as Caucasians from their primate ancestors. No wonder

Aborigines were brought to Britain and exhibited in cages as the missing link, or that Hitler, who had read Darwin, believed in his superior Aryan race!

Darwin was always unsure as to the merits of his work and often in his writings publicly confesses to his doubts concerning his theories.

> A brief summary will be sufficient to recall to the reader's mind the more salient points in this work. Many of the views which have been advanced are highly speculative, some no doubt will prove erroneous; but I have in every case given the reasons which have led me to one view rather than to another.[12]

He was aware that 'the conclusions arrived at in this work will be denounced by some as highly irreligious'.[13]

According to Thomas Huxley, Darwin's books had had a devastating impact on the teaching of the Church. He held the view that, despite his 'diligent search', he had found no defenders of the biblical story of Noah's 'deluge as being universal'. Bishop Barnes of Birmingham, preaching in Westminster Abbey, on 25 September 1927, expressed his view that 'Darwin's assertion that man has sprung from the apes has stood the test of more than half a century of critical examination.' He said, 'The stories of the creation of Adam and Eve, of their primal innocence and of their fall, have become for us folklore ... Darwin's triumph has destroyed the whole theological scheme.'[14] The Church of England in particular had taken on board a theory that was totally incompatible with the teaching of the Bible. To be fair to the Established Church, the theory had permeated the thinking of all denominations, with few exceptions.

Charles Darwin is often shown to be the man who may by the time of his death have believed in God and His act of creation; however, the following extracts from his writings show that that may be a false view. Darwin wrote in his biography:

> Disbelief crept over me at a very slow rate, but was at last complete. The rate was so slow that I felt no distress, and have never since doubted even for a single second that my conclusion was correct. I can indeed hardly see how anyone ought to wish

Christianity to be true; for if so the plain language of the text seems to show that the men who do not believe, and this would include my Father, Brother and almost all my best friends, will be everlastingly punished. And this is a damnable doctrine.[15]

This also shows Darwin was without the personal experience of the knowledge of God's love and grace shown in Jesus Christ.

In a letter from Darwin to N D Doedes of the University of Utrecht dated 2 April 1873, he wrote:

That the impossibility of conceiving that this grand and wondrous universe, with our conscious selves, arose through chance, seems to me the chief argument for the existence of God; but whether this is an argument of real value, I have never been able to decide. I am aware that if we admit a first cause, the mind still craves to know whence it came from and how it arose. Nor can I overlook the difficulty from the immense amount of suffering through the world. I am also induced to defer to a certain extent to the judgement of the many able men who have fully believed in God; but here again I see how poor an argument this is. The safest conclusion seems to be that the whole subject is beyond the scope of man's intellect; but man can do his duty.[16]

After studying Darwin's papers, Edward S Reed (*Darwin's Evolutionary Philosophy*) comes to this conclusion regarding his spirituality: 'Darwin was publicly satisfied to hint that God may have designed natural selection by breathing life into the first organism. Yet, privately, Darwin was unsatisfied to let God even create that first creature.'[17]

Shortly after the publication of his book *Origin*, Darwin wrote to his friend Sir Charles Lyell, and to the letter he added a postscript: 'Our ancestor was an animal which breathed water, had a swim bladder, a great swimming tail, an imperfect skull, and undoubtedly was a hermaphrodite! Here is a pleasant genealogy for mankind.'[18] Later, in *The Descent of Man*, he wrote:

I had two distinct objects in view; firstly, to shew that species had not been separately created, and secondly that natural selection had been the chief agent of change ... Some of those who admit the principle of evolution, but reject natural selection, seem to forget, when criticising my book, that I had the above objects in view; hence if I have erred in giving to natural selection great power, which I am far from admitting, or in having exaggerated its power, which is in itself probable, I have at least, as I hope, done good service in aiding to overthrow the dogma of separate creations.'[19]

According to Darwin, his belief in God receded gradually and by the time he came to write his biography he had come to the conclusion that he could no longer believe in the God of the Bible. Whether he ever had a personal faith in God is another matter. In his biography, he wrote, much to Emma's distress:

I gradually came to disbelieve in Christianity as a divine revelation. The fact that many false religions have spread over large portions of the earth like wild-fire had some weight with me. Beautiful as is the morality of the New Testament, it can hardly be denied that its perfection depends in part on the interpretation which we now put on metaphors and allegories.[20]

While this book is not primarily written to answer questions about suffering and the destiny of those who do not accept the Gospel, I can hardly ignore and fail to reply to Darwin's doubts. One has to wonder how well Darwin knew the contents of the Bible and whether he ever read its pages with any understanding. The Bible clearly explains that death, suffering and all that is wrong comes from the sin of our ancestor, Adam; more about that later. Darwin did not understand the Gospel, and he had not read or understood the words of the Gospel of John 3:16–17: 'For God so loved the world that he gave his one and only Son, that whoever believes in him shall not perish but have eternal life. For God did not send his Son into the world to condemn the world, but to save the world through him.' Why is it we often read verse 16 but not verse 17?

Dr Robert E D Clark, in his book *Darwin: Before and After*, gives a fascinating insight into Darwin's spiritual conflict. Remembering that Darwin had already admitted his ambition was 'to take a fair place among scientific men', we can see Clark goes to the very root of the problem:

It was a question of the praise of men or the praise of God, but he had already compromised himself so far that he could only choose the former.

To the end of his life, the old warfare continued in Darwin's mind. Try as he would, he could not escape from God. Gradually, his emotional life atrophied under the strain of the battle. Religious feeling disappeared and, with it, much else beside. Shakespeare was 'intolerably dull', he no longer took pleasure in pictures, in poetry, or even music. The beauty of nature no longer thrilled him. The world became cold and dead. As we have already seen, even his reasoning powers became distorted when he dwelt upon subjects even remotely concerned with his conflict.[21]

Emma and her sons had agreed that Charles would be buried at Downe, the place he loved. The local carpenter had made the unpolished coffin requested by the family. Scientists and politicians had other plans, much to the concern of Emma and her family. The Dean of Westminster agreed to their request that Darwin should be buried next to the great and famous in the Abbey. The rough coffin was replaced with a much grander affair. On 26 April 1882, pallbearers, including well-known evolutionists Thomas Huxley and Alfred Wallace, entered the Abbey, bearing the coffin of their protagonist, agnostic Charles Darwin.

Ten years later, C H Spurgeon, who was the greatest preacher in Britain during the second half of the nineteenth century, died while convalescing in the south of France. He was fiercely opposed to Darwin's teaching. During his pastorate at the Metropolitan Tabernacle, London, he baptised thousands of adults upon profession of faith in Jesus Christ. He established a host of societies to propagate the Gospel, an orphanage and a pastors' college. Under his leadership, the Baptists became a major denomination and a force for good in the country. His books and sermons (preached on occasion to 20,000 people) sold in the hundreds of thousands and were read by millions worldwide. He received no acclaim from scientists or politicians, and was not buried in a great church building, but thousands of ordinary men and women, whose lives had been changed by his Gospel preaching, lined the route of his funeral cortège to Norwood Cemetery. The Bible on top of the casket was the one

Spurgeon had so long preached from at the Tabernacle. It was opened at Isaiah 45:22: 'Look unto me and be saved, all you ends of the earth, for I am God, and there is no other.'

The contrast between the life and death of two prominent Victorians is remarkable. Darwin died consumed by self-doubt and he left a legacy of writings that influenced the thinking of atheistic philosophers. Their ideas would, in time, affect the thinking and programmes of tyrants in the twentieth century. The other, Spurgeon, who rejected evolution, brought joy, peace and relief from suffering to thousands, through his preaching at the Metropolitan Tabernacle. Spurgeon's influence continues today through his legacy of charities, books and sermons that are still widely read.

The attack of atheistic philosophy was successful – the Church bowed to evolutionary atheistic thinking. At the beginning of the twenty-first century, the Church as a body no longer teaches the foundational truths of Genesis 1–11; if it did there would be no need for some of the bodies that are mentioned in this book. A survey reported by a major national daily paper in December 1999 maintained that among the hundreds of leaders in several denominations in the UK, it found only three who actually believed the biblical account of creation. I have been unable to find one Anglican minister in my own diocese who believes in Adam and Eve as being real physical people, the creation by God having taken place during six twenty-four-hour day periods, and the flood having been universal. For many Christians the Bible begins with Abraham. Darwin's theory continues to make an overwhelming impact on philosophy, science, the media and the Church.

Notes

[1] Nicky Gumbel, *Searching Issues*, Kingsway Publications, 2001
[2] Charles Darwin, 1858, in a letter to a colleague regarding the concluding chapters of his *Origin of Species*. As quoted in 'John Lofton's Journal', *The Washington Times*, 8 February 1984. Cited by *The Revised Quote Book*, Creation Science Foundation Ltd, 1990, p.2
[3] C Darwin, *Voyage of the Beagle*, London, Penguin Classics, 1989, p.380

[4] C Darwin, *Autobiographies*, London, Penguin Classics, 1986, p.45
[5] Prayer written by the grandfather of Darwin's wife.
[6] C Darwin, *The Descent of Man*, London, Penguin Classics, 2004, pp.172–3
[7] Ibid., p.676
[8] Ibid., p.43
[9] C H Spurgeon, *Autobiography*, Passmore & Alabaster (in 4 vols), 1900
[10] Darwin, *The Descent of Man*, p.116
[11] Ibid., p.183–4
[12] Ibid., p.675
[13] Ibid., p.683
[14] Quoted by Ronald W Clark, *The Survival of Charles Darwin,* London, Weidenfeld & Nicolson, 1985, p.289
[15] Darwin, *Autobiographies*, p.50
[16] Quoted by Clark, *The Survival of Charles Darwin*, p.198
[17] Ibid. p.121
[18] Postscript of Charles Darwin's letter to Sir Charles Lyell, dated 10 January 1860, from Clark, *Survival of Charles Darwin*, p.121
[19] Darwin, *The Descent of Man*, p.81–2
[20] Darwin, *Autobiographies*, London, Penguin, p.49
[21] Dr Robert E D Clark, *Darwin: Before and After*, London, The Paternoster Press, 1958, p.93

Quotable Quotes

Darwin changed the life of the world ... We all believe that 'man is a monkey shaved' (Gilbert & Sullivan) ... Even the Pope accepts evolution.

Professor Steve Jones, *Start the Year*,
BBC Radio 4, 1 January 2001

The theory of evolution is universally accepted, not because it can be proved by logical, coherent evidence to be true, but because the only alternative, special creation, is clearly incredible.

Professor D M S Watson in *Nature*, vol. 124, p.233

I am astonished that you are so quickly deserting the one who called you by the grace of Christ and are turning to a different gospel – which really is no gospel at all. Evidently some people are throwing you into confusion and are trying to pervert the gospel of Christ. But even if we or an angel from heaven should preach a gospel other than the one we preached to you, let him be eternally condemned! As we have already said, so now I say again: If anybody is preaching to you a gospel other than what you accepted, let him be eternally condemned!

Galatians 1:6–9

Jacob said to his father, 'I am Esau, your first born. I have done as you told me. Please sit up and eat some of my game so that you may give me your blessing.'

Genesis 27:19 (a good example of deception)

There is not a shred of conclusive evidence for the ancestry of man: the whole structure of its colossal delusion rests upon certain similarities between the physical nature of man and that of the animals – similarities which are easily explainable without postulating any descent of man from the apes.

George H Bonner, 'The Case against Evolution'
in *Nineteenth Century*, 1927, p.593

'The fool hath said in his heart', etc. It is in his heart he says this; this is the secret desire of every unconverted bosom. If the breast of God were within reach of men, it would be stabbed a million times in one moment. When God was manifest in flesh, he was altogether lovely; he did no sin; he went about continually doing good: and yet they took him and hung him on a tree; they mocked him and spat upon him. And this is the way men would do with God again. Learn first, the depravity of your heart … Secondly, the amazing love of Christ – 'While we were enemies, Christ died for us.'

Robert Murray M'Cheyne, 1813–1843,
commenting on Psalm 53

II

The Great Deception –
a Warning from the Bible

Jesus Christ taught that preceding His imminent return to Earth there will be a great deception of the Church. The Apostles also added their warnings. Paul warned Timothy that the Holy Spirit tells us clearly that in the last times some in the Church will turn away from Christ and become eager followers of teachers with Devil-inspired ideas. These teachers will tell lies with straight faces and do it so often that their consciences won't even bother them (see 1 Timothy 4:1–2 and compare 2 Peter 2:1–3).

The Greek word *pseudologos*, translated here as 'teachers that tell lies', means literally 'false word', in contrast to the Lord Jesus Christ who is the true *logos*, 'true word'.

The American theologian Wilbur Smith, commenting on these verses wrote:

> Here is something remarkable – that men who teach lies are prophesied as appearing with greatest power and frequency in the very days, the last of this age, when scientific and historical knowledge has advanced so greatly! ... These are not ignorant teachers, nor dull teachers, but false teachers. I do not know that there is any more terrible verse in the New Testament than Timothy 4:1, which tell us that these men are actually under the power of seducing spirits, and will be teaching the doctrines advanced by demons themselves. It is a startling thing to say, but it is according to the Word of God, that men who teach falsely concerning the Lord Jesus Christ, who pervert the truths of the New Testament, who deny God's revelation concerning His Son, who repudiate the cardinal doctrines of the Christian faith – these men, however learned, however polished, however suave, however powerful of speech, are men under the control of seducing spirits and demons.[1]

John Metcalfe has made this comment in his book *Creation*, on these verses of the Apostle Paul to Timothy:

> Furthermore on a different level I have presented the witness of a substantial number of eminent scientists, each one of whom gives the lie to evolutionary uniformitarianism.
>
> The truth is that in the last days a blinding delusion has come upon mankind for the exceeding wickedness that covers the earth, and fills Christendom. A great part of this delusion lies in the spirit that has swept over the compulsory educational system under the falsely so called name of science, denying the Creation.
>
> These vast changes of comparatively recent origin are nothing but the very signs preceding and leading up to the end of the world. This is the time for the people of God to take heed, abiding steadfast in the unchanged and unchangeable word of God ... Moreover it is clear that in little more than the past century, titanic forces of deception have been let loose upon a godless and willing mankind, and in an apostate and complacent church. This is the fulfilment in the latter times of what was spoken expressly by the Spirit in the beginning, that there should be a departure from the faith in consequence of the activity of seducing spirits, 1 Timothy 4:1.
>
> Because of the mounting iniquity and towering godlessness manifest up to and over the past few generations, the restraints laid by Almighty God upon the degree to which the world could be deceived by the mystery of iniquity have been removed, 2 Thessalonians 2:7.
>
> These have gone, and the mystery of iniquity – for over a century – has worked unchecked, pervading the world and its various systems more and more openly, 2 Thessalonians 2:3–10. This in turn has resulted in a blinding – and strong – delusion, that the world, and fallen religion, should believe a lie, for now it is certain that they will not receive the love of the truth, 2 Thessalonians 2:11–12.[2]

It is incredible that so many within and outside the Church should have been so convincingly deceived by what is only an unproven theory, which over 150 years has found no scientific evidence for its support.

Not only does the Apostle Paul warn about a great deception in the last days but also the Apostle Peter, who writes to the

Church, 'In the last days scoffers will come, scoffing and follow-ing their own evil desires. They will say, "Where is this 'coming' he promised? Ever since our fathers died, everything goes on as it has since the beginning of creation." ' (2 Peter 3:3–4). Here is a clear indication that Peter accepted the Genesis record of creation. Peter exposes the error that since the beginning the world all has been as it is – unchanged. There were people in the Apostolic Church who denied that there had been a worldwide flood. The 'theory of uniformitarianism' teaches that there has been uni-formity for billions of years – no change in the ratios of substances in the Earth's rocks and atmosphere, e.g. carbon-14, uranium-thorium, potassium-argon, helium, etc. Uniformitari-anism is also called the 'closed system'. The uniformitarian doctrine teaches that the Earth has undergone very slow change through erosion and deposition and denies the huge upheavals that have taken place that the Bible so clearly teaches. Teaching of this doctrine has no scientific basis, and is the reason for the wild calculations of the Earth's age. Christians today should take heed of Peter's prophetic warning, which I believe is particularly relevant to any debate on evolutionary teaching in the Church in our day.

The Apostle Peter writing to the Church (2 Peter 3:3–6) confirms the Genesis account of creation, particularly Genesis 1:6–8, 'And God said, "Let there be an expanse between the waters to separate water from water." So God made the expanse and separated the water under the expanse from the water above it. And it was so. God called the expanse "sky".' This is the only part of the creation that God did not say was good; this is because this water vapour was to deluge the Earth in God's judgement, which we know changed our planet. However, Peter is warning against those who believe in the theory of uniformitarianism and who refuse to acknowledge the teaching of Scripture. Peter continues his discourse by reminding those who refuse to believe the Scriptures that they will be judged. So many have been deceived over the centuries, which has only led them into making wrong decisions and reaping the consequences.

How are we being deceived?

In the New Testament, we are warned over ninety times by Jesus and His Apostles to be on guard against deceivers. It will become clear who some of those arrogant teachers are, as we further explore this subject of deception.

The Oxford English Dictionary defines the verb to deceive as: 'To ensnare, to take unawares by craft or guile, to overcome, overreach, or get the better of by trickery, or beguile or betray into mischief or sin; to mislead, to cause to believe what is false; to mislead as to matter of fact, lead into error, impose upon, delude.'

The deception I refer to is the teaching of the theory of evolution as fact, in whatever guise it is taught. Christians especially are being misled about matters of fact. We are caused to believe what is false and in doing so we are being led into error. Before Darwin's *Theory of Evolution* was published (1859), few doubted the truth of the Genesis account of creation, the fall of man, or Noah's flood. They were all considered to be events that took place and were recorded by God. Most people had a regard for an almighty God, although they may not have attended a church.

Henri Blocher, in his book *In the Beginning* (1984), writes about those who hold the literal view of Genesis:

> This is the reading that enjoys the support of the majority throughout church history, notably that of the Reformers. Competent, authoritative commentators have followed it, such as C F Keil in the nineteenth century and E J Young in this century. Mention may also be made of the Australian, Noel Weeks, and of the scientists associated with the Creation Research Society (with J C Whitcomb filling the theological role). They are all agreed that the days are to be taken in the ordinary sense and that the narrative aims to give us the chronology of the work of creation. It is quite simply history.[3]

Many people find it difficult to reconcile what they were taught about evolution (whether it was by Christians or unbelievers) with Scripture. Some believe that perhaps there was another world before the one mentioned in Genesis chapters one and two, or perhaps the six days were millions of years. Or that there was a 'gap' between verses one and two of Genesis 1 of millions of years. A few years ago I was invited by a friend to attend a day seminar organised by a well-known central London church. The speaker repeated several times a statement that made me think: 'There was no death until Adam sinned.' So what about fossils found that supposedly pre-date humans? I asked myself. This led me on to explore the Genesis text, reading what the leading scholars have said about its construction, reliability and interpretation. I had access to a huge number of books at the Evangelical Library in London. I had heard Professor E J Young speak on the Hebrew text when at college and was now able to read again his book on Genesis. I am now convinced that the text of Genesis is intended to be interpreted literally and it is honouring God to do so. Since I adopted this position, every time I have answered questions from this viewpoint put by seeking people, they have listened more intently and have been more willing to open up to hearing the Gospel. Previously I had tried to make Genesis chapters 1–11 compatible with atheistic evolutionary teaching. I found people wanted to hear other views. Since rejecting wholeheartedly the teaching of macroevolution and natural selection I have found that a great cloud has been lifted from my mind and spirit. To God be the Glory.

Evolution is the unproven theory that all life forms originated from the same single cell. It is important to distinguish between macroevolution and microevolution. Macroevolution is the theory that one species can become another. Microevolution is the variation that can be found in the same species. The genetic information is already there to enable the variation in variety. Most who believe in the biblical account of creation (Genesis 1 & 2) accept microevolution. In this book the word 'evolution' refers to man originating from another species such as fish or apes.

If we are to speak to anyone about creation, and counter error that has been sown in their minds, we must understand for ourselves the foundations of our faith, which are laid in the first chapters of Genesis. Jesus and the Apostles referred to these chapters and we do well to understand how important and foundational they are to all the teaching that follows on from the Patriarchs and through into the other books of the Bible. When the Apostle Paul spoke to Gentiles in Athens (Acts 17), he took a different starting point from the Apostle Peter when he spoke to Jews who were knowledgeable about the one true God, Jehovah. Paul pointed to creation and quoted their poets. He then told them about the world and the unknown God who was responsible for all that was created. He concluded by narrating how this God had personally made himself known in Jesus Christ and who had died on the cross for sinners.

Christians need to understand how the teaching of evolution over time has permeated the thinking of our nation, and especially how it has affected how the Church presents the Gospel. It has lowered the moral standards in the life of the Church because we no longer accept the two universal rules God laid down in the first chapters of Genesis: the true nature of marriage being between those of the opposite sex for life; and that we should observe the day set aside for worship and rest. Atheistic evolution has become ingrained into our culture, so much so that anyone who thinks differently is considered intolerant and a dangerous fundamentalist. If the person is a Christian they may be considered to have strayed spiritually. This is due to many people in authority in our churches not knowing what creationists believe because they have never studied special creation. The Church has been seriously weakened by the teaching of theistic evolution and the rejection of the first chapters of the Book of Genesis as a factual account.

John Mulinde, in his book *Set Apart for God*, acknowledges how the culture in which we have been raised is often a brake put on the proclamation of the Gospel. Our very culture often limits the boundaries of our evangelism. Furthermore, when the Church adopts the morals of our culture, the world cannot see the One we represent because of sin within the Church:

> There are strongholds deeply and manifestly entrenched in the lifestyles of people in every region of the world. These are so deeply rooted that it appears almost impossible to bring communities to the point where they can experience God's glorious power of revival. There are so many things that stand in the way of genuine nation-sweeping revivals, such as culture, tradition, mindsets, indulgent lifestyles and the general worldview of

people today. I was profoundly aware of how the nations, and their peoples – including even the Christian believers – are held in captivity to their social systems. These bondages have become so much a part of us that we scarcely notice how they cause our lives to *differ from what is in the Word of God. Instead, we conform to the world around us.*[4]

The theory of evolution and all that follows from it has become ingrained in our culture and is the major obstacle we have to overcome when preaching the Gospel. The teaching of atheistic evolutionary thought over a century has dulled the minds and hearts of our population so much that they feel no prick of conscience for sin any longer. There is no expectation that one day they will have to face the living God. Death means the end of consciousness to most people – after that, nothing!

Notes

[1] Wilbur Smith, *World Crisis and the Prophetic Scriptures*, Chicago, Moody Press, 1952, pp.300–301
[2] John Metcalfe, *Creation*, John Metcalfe Publishing Trust, November 1996, pp.21–23
[3] Henri Blocher, *In the Beginning*, Inter-Varsity Press, 1984, p.46
[4] John Mulinde, *Set Apart from God*, Sovereign World International, 2005, p.16

Quotable Quotes

If some things were never meant to be shared, then it is not surprising to learn that there are times when even God refuses to share. He is a loving and merciful God who loves to pour out his mercy and grace on his people. But there are some things that he will not share. This is especially true when it comes to the prerogatives of his deity. God will not share his glory with any other god. So he has given us this command: 'You shall have no other gods before me' (Exodus 20:3). This is the fundamental commandment, the one that comes before all the others and lays the foundation for them. Before we learn anything else about what God demands, we need to know who he is and who we are in relationship to him. 'Now get this straight,' God is saying, 'I am the one and only God. And since I am the only God, I refuse to share my worship with anyone or anything else.' God will not share the stage with any other performers. He refuses to have any colleagues. He will not even acknowledge that he has any genuine rivals. God does not simply lay claim to one part of our life and worship; he demands that we dedicate all we are and all we have to his service and praise. Thus the Ten Commandments begin by asserting the great theological principle of *soli Deo gloria*: glory to God alone.

> Philip Graham Ryken, *Written in Stone,*
> *The Ten Commandments and Today's Moral Crisis*,
> Wheaton, Crossway Books, 2003, pp.57–58

Evolution is basically a religious philosophy. We in creation ministries are explaining to people that both creation and evolution are religious views of life upon which people build their particular models of philosophy, science, or history. The issue, therefore, is not science versus religion, but religion versus religion (the science of one religion versus the science of another religion).

> Ken Ham, *The Lie: Evolution*, Green Forest AR,
> Master Books, 1987, p.32

And God spoke all these words: 'I am the Lord your God, who brought you out of Egypt, out of the land of slavery. You shall have no other gods before me.'

Exodus 20:1–2

Can a mortal be more righteous than God? Can a man be more pure than his Maker?

Job 4:17

Today, evolution still stands primarily for an attitude of mind – and it is a dangerous and ugly one at that. It encourages pride and excitement which eventually lead to disillusionment and loss of peace of mind. It focuses attention on wild schemes for improvement which never materialise and make men lose a sense of their limitations ... Above all, the so-called 'evolutionary outlook' is still exactly what Darwin made it – a substitute god. Though evolution is accepted by moderns chiefly as a means for repressing their religious needs. We are told on all hands that the modern man cannot believe in God because it is 'unscientific' to do so or just because he cannot imagine what God is like.

Dr Robert E D Clark, *Darwin: Before and After*, London, Paternoster Press, 1958, p.187

III

Evolution is a Religious Faith

Ken Ham, in his book *The Lie: Evolution*, writes:

> Evolution is a religious position that makes human opinion supreme. As we shall see, its fruits (because of rejection of the Creator and Lawgiver) are lawlessness, immorality, impurity, abortion, racism, and a mocking of God. Creation is a religious position based on the Word of God and its fruits (through God's Spirit) are love, joy, peace, patience, kindness, goodness, faithfulness, gentleness, and self-control. The creation/evolution issue (is God Creator?) is the crux of the problems in our society today. It is the fundamental issue with which Christians must come to grips. The creation/evolution issue is where the battle really rages.[1]

The theory of evolution has had a powerful effect on our thinking for 150 years. Even though later we shall see that major scientific discoveries of recent days prove the theory to be untenable, it is a remarkable fact that its advocates still remain committed to its propagation with as great a fervour as ever. Every evolutionist waits with faith (a 'faith' that would make most Christians ashamed) for some concrete evidence that a great genetic leap has been made by one species to become another (macroevolution).

Every religion has a moral code. Jesus taught, 'Love the Lord your God with all your heart, with all your soul and with all your mind. Love your neighbour as yourself.' Jesus made the further comment that all 'the Law and the Prophets hang on these two commandments'. Matthew Henry (1662–1714) comments, 'This is the sum and substance of all those precepts relating to practical religion which were written by Moses (the Pentateuch), and backed and enforced by the preaching and writing of the prophets.' Only Jesus who, with the Father and Holy Spirit, was at creation, had the authority to make a statement of that magnitude about God's love, the Law and the Prophets.

The Gospel we read about in the Bible is the Good News of God's sacrificial love for us. The gospel of evolution is about life and death, the survival of the fittest and the need for physical death in order that man can perhaps evolve by reproduction into eventual perfection.

How the *Theory of Evolution* has blinded people's views on morality

What moral code have we inherited from the atheistic promoters of the *Theory of Evolution*? Francis Schaeffer wrote:

> Darwin's idea was popularised by Thomas Huxley (1825–1895). Herbert Spencer (1820–1903), who actually coined the phrase 'survival of the fittest', extended the theory of biological evolution to all of life, including ethics. Spencer said, 'The poverty of the incapable … starvation of the idle and those shoulderings aside of the weak by the strong … the decrees of a large, far-seeing benevolence.' There was no necessity to extend biological evolution to 'social Darwinism'. But it was natural for these men to do this because of their desire to find a unifying principle that would enable autonomous man to explain everything through naturalistic science, that is, on the basis of the uniformity of natural causes in a closed system. This had become the frame of reference by which they attempted to give unity to individual things, the particulars, to the details of the universe and to the history of man. In *Physics and Politics: Thoughts on the Application of Principles of Natural Selection and Inheritance to Political Science* (1872), Walter Bagehot (1826–1877) went even further than Spencer in applying these concepts to the advance of groups. Thus these concepts opened the door for racism and the non-compassionate use of accumulated wealth to be sanctioned and made respectable in the name of 'science'. Later, these ideas helped produce an even more far-reaching yet logical conclusion, the Nazi movement in Germany.[2]

Perhaps more controversial than *Origin* was Darwin's book *The Descent of Man*. In this book Darwin was determined to consider, 'firstly, whether man, like every other species, is descended from some pre-existing form; secondly, the manner of his development; and thirdly, the value of differences between the so-called races of man'.[3] He came to the conclusion that man is descended from some 'lowly-organised form'. Although other atheists had touched similarly on this subject, Darwin's book was more persuasive. He hoped that his book had 'at least, as I hope, done good service in aiding to overthrow the dogma of separate creations'.[4] Perhaps this book more than *Origin* was to be the stepping stone to 'eugenics', the science of race improvement.

Thomas F Heinze, in his *Creation vs. Evolution Handbook*, writes:

> Evolution today has an influence far beyond simply being used as an explanation of the origin of the species. It has been imposed upon many areas of life ... That which interests us the most here is the area of morality. Evolution provides man with a way to escape his responsibility to God. If everything in existence today has developed without God, then there is no judge before whom we must all appear. In the interpretation of many, man is responsible only to himself, that which helps evolution helps society. Hitler used this [theory of evolution] to rationalise his hatred of the Jews.[5]

I refer again to Thomas F Heinze's *Creation vs. Evolution Handbook*:

> Using evolution as his rationalisation Hitler guided one of the most advanced nations the world has ever known in the massacre of millions of people, of whom many were women and children, almost all of whom were innocent of any crime against him or his government ... There is often a real difference between the conduct of one who is convinced that God exists and that he is responsible to Him, as he tries to obey God's command to love even his enemies and to treat them as he would like to be treated, and the conduct of one who does not believe in God [like Hitler], but thinks that it would be best for the race to eliminate whomever he happens to consider inferior.[6]

It is not surprising, therefore, to learn that Hitler's regime resorted to introduce legislation which would decide which people would be allowed to reproduce and later to live. In July 1933 the Sterilisation Law was implemented, and in the first year of legislation nearly 400,000 people were investigated by the Hereditary Health Courts, who decided 62,000 people should be sterilised. All that was necessary for a doctor to show was that the person investigated was 'feeble-minded' or had one of nine congenital conditions.

Two years later, the science of eugenics was enshrined in the Law for the Protection of German Blood and German Honour. It outlawed marriage and sexual intercourse between 'Germans and related blood' and Jews.

Sir Arthur Keith (1866–1955), an eminent scientist and author of books on human embryology, morphology and anthropology, came to the conclusion that the only explanation for Hitler's behaviour was that he was an 'uncompromising evolutionist'. In *Mein Kampf* (1933), Hitler made his views very clear and they were put into action in his treatment of Jews, gypsies and those whom he and his cohorts considered unsuitable for reproductive purposes – as we now know, millions were disposed of in the most brutal way. During the war, Alfred Rosenberg drew up for Hitler rules for the National Reich Church that would have control of all churches. Only National Reich orators would preach; the Bible would be replaced on the communion table by *Mein Kampf* and, on its left, a sword. The Christian cross was replaced with the swastika. Presumably, Hitler's intention was to act as a god or to take the place of God. The text of Rosenberg's document appears in the book *It's your Souls We Want* by Stewart W Herman, who was Pastor of the American Church in Berlin during the years 1936–1941. Rosenberg was found guilty of war crimes at Nuremberg and executed with others on 16 October 1946.

It is only a small step from eugenics to euthanasia. The Netherlands introduced legislation in 2001 enshrining euthanasia into their law for those with terminal illnesses. We should be thankful to Dame Cicely Saunders and the hospice movement for bringing love, compassion and a holistic approach to those who suffer through terminal illness. There are thousands who would testify to the care they received at a hospice. If we have lost the tenderness to love and care for the ill, those who have physical or learning difficulties or those who hunger and thirst in the Third World, then we can only expect the condemnation of a righteous God. Jesus' own words alert us to being complacent and indicate how we shall be judged:

> Lord, when did we see you hungry and feed you, or thirsty and give you something to drink? When did we see you a stranger and invite you in, or needing clothes and clothe you? When did we see you sick or in prison and go to visit you?' The King will reply, 'I tell you the truth, whatever you did for one of the least of these brothers of mine, you did for me.' Then he will say to those on his left, 'Depart from me, you who are cursed, into eternal fire prepared for the devil and his angels. For I was hungry and you gave me nothing to eat. I was thirsty and you gave me nothing to drink. I was a stranger and you did not invite me in. I needed clothes and you did not clothe me, I was sick and in prison and you did not look after me.' They will answer, 'Lord, when did we see you hungry or thirsty or a stranger or needing clothes or sick or in prison and did not help you?' He will reply, 'I tell you the truth, whatever you did not do for one of the least of these, you did not do for me.' Then they will go away to eternal punishment, but the righteous to eternal life.

Matthew 25:37–46

It is not surprising to learn that not only was Hitler influenced by Darwin's writings, but so were Stalin and Mao Tse-tung, who both inflicted such dreadful brutality on their own peoples. Far more people in the twentieth century have been slaughtered and injured by man than by natural disasters.

The Bible teaches that God is the ultimate judge of all people. Christians worldwide, and especially the persecuted Church, look for His promise to be fulfilled:

> Just as man is destined to die once, and after that to face judgement, so Christ was sacrificed once to take away the sin of many people; *and he will appear a second time, not to bear sin, but to bring salvation to those who are waiting for him.*

Hebrews 9:27–28 (italics my emphasis)

A decline in moral standards

Atheistic evolutionary teaching has created a climate of thinking where an 'amoral code' is produced by a consensus of public opinion gathered by means of random selectivity. I wrote to the Independent Television Commission (ITC) (now absorbed into the regulator OFCOM) about programmes which showed nudity and sexual acts.

This is an extract from the reply:

> A body such as ITC must attempt to reflect public opinion in general. For better or worse, the days when Lord Reith could impose his own views on the output of the BBC are long gone. Much late night programming is not by any means to my taste but it is not for me to impose my views on other adults who may choose to watch provided that the material is harmless and unlikely to offend those watching at that time. The introduction of the Human Rights Act has emphasised again that freedom of expression must be given due consideration and denied only when necessary.

Is it harmless? *The Jerry Springer Show* has engendered even more hatred and anger between spouses. It has been alleged that one dispute resulted in murder. *Jerry Springer: The Opera* with its endless profanities was shown on BBC TV. This was in the face of 50,000 letters of complaint and demonstrations outside the offices of the corporation. The BBC seems to have forgotten that revenues come from many followers of Jesus Christ who do not want their licence fees used for programmes that do not honour their leader. Is it not time that the Government privatised the BBC, and gave shares to the licence holders from the sale? The BBC should raise capital like any other channel. Furthermore millions of Christians in the UK seem to have forgotten God's gift of writing – or have they adopted ITC standards? Ask Care for their media card now (email@care.org.uk). Take one hour a week to congratulate or complain. From a reply to my letter to Channel 4 concerning *Eurotrash* (this programme once followed *Frasier* at 10.30 p.m.), I quote their last paragraph: '…we cannot give you the assurance that you seek, that we intend to eliminate nudity and sexual acts from this programme. I am sorry I can't be more positive.' According to a BBC *Panorama* programme there is much worse yet to be shown on our TV sets in the very near future. *Big Brother* was just the start!

As a nation, we no longer subscribe to the code of morals, originally written in stone, called the Ten Commandments. These moral laws are today considered obsolete and are brushed aside and seldom considered in our society. There are no absolutes in our society any more. The creator God made them for our benefit. Later they were confirmed by the life and teaching of Jesus Christ. Asked what was the greatest commandment, Jesus replied:

> Love the Lord your God with all your heart and with all your soul and with all your mind. This is the first and greatest commandment. And the second is like it: Love your neighbour as yourself. All the Law and the Prophets hang on these two commandments.

> Matthew 22:37–40

As atheistic evolutionary teaching has permeated our thinking, society has ceased to believe in an ultimate judge (God), and only believes in the rule of 'public opinion', however debased it may become. Indescribable filth can be screened on TV while Christian bodies are denied by Act of Parliament the right to national broadcasting licences. One Christian TV programmer was fined for quoting Scripture that referred to homosexuality! Evolution is a religion that has no absolutes, and can bring no hope. A great number of schools in our nation do not practise the mandatory observance of an act of worship or teach biblical Christianity, and yet the religion of atheistic evolution is advanced every time geology, science or physiology is taught, with few exceptions. Pray that God will deliver we who call ourselves Christians from the delusion of atheistic evolutionary theories, which unfortunately have had a profound influence on our thinking on special creation and moral issues.

Notes

[1] Ken Ham, *The Lie: Evolution*, Green Forest AR, Master Books, 1987, p.29

[2] Dr Francis A Schaffer, *How Then Should We Live?*, New Jersey, Fleming H Revell Co., 1976, pp.150–151

[3] Darwin, *The Descent of Man*, Introduction, p.18

[4] Darwin, *The Descent of Man*, chapter 2, p.82

[5] Thomas F Heinze, *Creation vs. Evolution Handbook*, Grand Rapids MI, Baker Publishing Group, 1988, pp.99–100

[6] Ibid., pp.100–101

Weekend Reading from the Select Bibliography

Darwin and Darwinism 150 Years Later –
Biblical Faith and the Christian Worldview,
Ian McNaughton and Paul Taylor,
Day One Publications, 2009

The authors look at the life of Charles Darwin, his early life and education, through to his burial at Westminster Abbey. They examine his religious ideas and why his book *On the Origin of Species* has had a profound impact on the Western world to this very day. I found this book easy to read and the notes at the end of each chapter helpful.

Part Two

Quotable Quotes

THE LORD GOD SPEAKS TO JOB

Then the Lord answered Job out of the storm. He said: Who is this that darkens my counsel with words without knowledge? Brace yourself like a man; I will question you, and you shall answer me. Where were you when I laid the earth's foundation? Tell me, if you understand. Who marked off its dimensions? Surely you know! Who stretched a measuring line across it? On what were its footings set, or who laid its cornerstone – while the morning stars sang together and all the angels shouted for joy? … Will the one who contends with the Almighty correct him? Let him who accuses God answer him! Then Job answered the Lord: 'I am unworthy – how can I reply to you? I put my hand over my mouth. I spoke once but I have no answer – twice, but I will say no more.'

Job 38:1–7; 40:2–5

Then, when you come to the intellectuals, we are told that they are now scientific in their outlook, that they accept the theory of evolution and the entire scientific outlook which makes a three-dimensional world impossible, etc., and that therefore we must make it plain to them that the Bible only deals with matters of salvation and religious experience and living. If we fail to show that the Bible and Nature (as expounded by scientists) are complementary and equally authoritative forms of revelation we shall offend this modern intellectualist and he will not even listen to the Gospel. So we must stop talking, as we have done in the past, about the origin of the world and of man, about the fall, and about miracles and supernatural interventions in history, and we must concentrate only on this religious message.

Dr Martyn Lloyd-Jones, *Preaching and Preachers*, London,
Hodder & Stoughton, 1974, pp.124–5

Who has gone up to heaven and come down?
Who has cupped the wind in the palms of his hands?
Who has wrapped up the waters in his cloak?
Who established all the ends of the earth?
What is his name, and what is his son's names?
Surely you know!
Every word of God's is pure; he shields those taking refuge in him.

Proverbs 30:4–5, *The Complete Jewish Bible*

IV

We Have Become Conditioned to Evolutionary Thinking

How many of these twelve statements do you believe to be true?

1. The Earth is 12 billion years old
2. Man evolved from sea creatures
3. Everything started with a 'chance' Big Bang
4. Adam and Eve and the fall are just myths that explain a spiritual truth
5. The Bible account of the flood was just a local flood
6. Dinosaurs lived 60 million years before man
7. The Book of Genesis chapters 1–11 are not scientific
8. Cain had no one to marry
9. The Book of Genesis tells you why, not how
10. Carbon dating methods are reliable
11. God used evolution in order to make man
12. We are descended from hominids

Most of these statements arise from the delusion that evolution by way of the Big Bang hypothesis and natural selection is the way men, women and our universe have come about over billions of years. Answer to statement 8: read Genesis 5, verse 4. After this section you may want to revise your score! What about the Big Bang theory? Read on!

Einstein and other scientists, in seeking to apply his theory of general relativity to the universe, have assumed that matter is spread uniformly throughout space. This assumption – known as the Cosmological Principle – became the foundation for the standard big bang model describing the origin and evolution of the universe. But with modern technology (e.g. the Hubble Space Telescope) astronomers have now observed substantially more of the universe than in Einstein's day, and as they peer into space the universe appears anything but uniform. Galaxies are gathered together in great chains and walls which curl around vast regions of empty space known as 'voids'. But most cosmologists are still clinging to the hope that the universe is 'smooth' on large scales. As the Professor of Astrophysics at Nottingham University acknowledges, once they accept that the universe is not uniform, 'We're lost … The foundations of the big bang models would crumble away. We'd be left with no explanation for the big bang or galaxy formation, or the distribution of galaxies in the universe.'[1]

Francis A Schaeffer, in his book *Genesis in Space and Time*, writing on the Big Bang, puts the views of Bible-believing Christians very clearly:

A few years ago in England some Christians became excited about the Big Bang theory, thinking that it favoured Christianity. But they really missed the point – either the point of Scripture or the Big Bang theory or both. The simple fact is that what is given in Genesis 1:1 has no relationship to the Big Bang theory – because from the scriptural viewpoint, the primal creation goes back beyond the basic material or energy. We have a new thing created by God out of nothing by fiat [an authoritative order], and this is the distinction.[2]

The Eternal One controls time!

Sometimes the verse 'with the Lord a day is like a thousand years' (2 Peter 3:8) is quoted to support millions of years and the theory of evolution, but in its context this verse refers to God's patience. Peter is quoting from Psalm 90, verses 3 and 4: 'You bring frail mortals to the point of being crushed, then say, "People, Repent!" For from your viewpoint a thousand years are merely like yesterday or a night watch' (*Complete Jewish Bible*). It illustrates that He is a God who has infinite patience with man. Another truth that we sometimes forget is that God is 'outside time'. God created the flow of time in our cosmology as we now experience it. We are designed to live within that time cycle of rest and work: a twenty-four-hour day, seven-day week, six days for work and a day to rest and worship God. God is not caught in a time capsule as we are. Eternity is a state of being, not an endless duration of time. Eternal life is not endless life but a new state of living without time. There will be no need for clocks in heaven. The mystery of the incarnation is that the eternal God came as a man subject to the limitation of time. Jesus said, 'In the beginning at the time of Creation, God made them male and female' (Mark 10:6, *Good News Bible*). Time began for our world on the first day of creation and for man on day six. Earth time, to which we are subject, is due to the rotation of the Earth and its relative position to the sun at any given moment. In His wisdom God created man biologically to fit into this time system and He thought 'it was good' to do so. When astronauts go into space, they are still subject to the 'twenty-four-hour clock' that God built into us! There is no reason why we should not believe God used this same 'time clock' from day one of creation. He didn't need the sun or stars to make this calculation; He could do it Himself.

In his book *Thy Word is Truth*, E J Young, commenting on the text from Apostle Peter's letter, writes, 'In these words the Lord tells us that He is not bound by time. "Before the mountains were brought forth, or ever thou hadst formed the earth and the world, even from everlasting to everlasting, thou *art* God." [Psalm 90:2]' (*Authorised Version*).[3]

Another Bible truth we do well to remember is that God said, 'I AM THAT I AM' (Exodus 3:14, *Authorised Version*), 'signifies that He is self-existent, the only real being and the source of all reality; that He is eternal and unchangeable in His promises'.[4]

The teaching of evolution undermines the teaching of both the Old and New Testaments. If the teaching of the Old Testament (OT) is undermined, then so is the New Testament. Without the Old there cannot be the New! Jesus and the Apostles quoted the OT, including Genesis; and the prophecies concerning our salvation are to be found starting in the early chapters of Genesis (3:15). Helen Shapiro, the pop star, was convinced that Jesus was the Messiah promised by God because He fulfilled all the OT prophecies. Helen would agree that without her study of the OT she would never have put her faith in Jesus, whose ministry is recorded in the New Testament, and taken Him as her personal Saviour and Lord.

If God did not create Adam and Eve as real people and we are a product of evolution, there is no need for a saviour from sin in Christ Jesus, as there is no afterlife; in fact we are without hope (read 1 Corinthians 15:14–19). If we evolved from hominids then there was no fall from grace and no need for a redeemer. If there is no God to be accountable to, then we may choose our own standards! Interviewed on BBC Radio 4, Professor Peter Atkins said, 'Science is truth, there is no meaning to life.'[5] What a sad thought for the start of any day!

Notes

[1] *Creation ex Nihilo*, vol. 22, no. 1, p.8: Editorial referring to *New Scientist*, 21/8/1999, pp.23–36, and *Science*, 16/4/1999, pp.445–6

[2] Francis A Schaeffer, *Genesis in Space and Time*, London, Hodder & Stoughton, 1973, p.28

[3] E J Young, *Thy Word is Truth*, Edinburgh, The Banner of Truth Trust, 1997, p.168

[4] Dr E F Kevan, *The New Bible Commentary*, ed. by Professor F Davidson, London, The Inter-Varsity Fellowship, 1953, p.109

[5] Professor Peter Atkins, *Today* programme, 1 November 2000

Quotable Quotes

God's sacred Word among us; which is that inestimable treasure, which excelleth all the riches of the earth; because the fruit thereof extendeth itself, not only to the time spent in this transitory world, but directeth and disposeth men unto that eternal happiness which is above in heaven.

'The Epistle Dedicatory', *Authorised Version (KJV)*, AD 1611

This Book [the Bible] is, the most valuable thing that this world affords. Here is Wisdom; this is the royal Law; these are the lively Oracles of God.

From the Coronation Service of
Her Majesty Queen Elizabeth II, 2 June 1953

The opening verses of the Bible are simply astounding! Such seemingly simple sentences, which we often take for granted, are loaded with grand biblical truths. These are plain statements that refute much of today's false teaching. Firstly, they deny *atheism*, for the one God created everything. Secondly, they deny *pantheism* (the belief that a god is in all things and all people), for God is transcendent, above and beyond creation. Thirdly, they deny *polytheism*, for only one God made the universe. Fourthly, they deny *humanism*, for God and not man is on the throne of the universe. Fifthly, they deny *evolution*, because man did not develop from the primordial soup, but he was specially created by the one true God. And, frankly, that is why there is meaning to life. That is why those who believe in God can say that our chief reason for existence is to glorify him and enjoy him for ever. If this God is the Creator, then we are to live for his glory! As the apostle John declares, 'Worthy are you, our Lord and our God, to receive glory and honour and power; for you created all things, and because of your will they existed, and were created.' (Revelation 4:11)

Dr John D Currid, *Study Commentary on Genesis*, Darlington,
Evangelical Press, 2003, vol. 1, p.64

While studying with Francis Schaeffer in the summer of 1977, I acquired the term 'true truth'. Dr Schaeffer coined this term because of the lack of respect the word *truth* commands in our day. He said it was not a tautology but a necessity. The absolutes, including those in the first chapters of Genesis, are not up for election. They are not running in any ballot, except in the imaginary constructs in men's minds. I know this well, because quite a few of these mental images were floating around in my own mind in 1975. It was in that year that the Truth set me free from my sin and began to set me free from these mental images concerning the beginning of mankind.

Dr Jack Cuozzo, 'Orthodontics', quoted in Dr D Ashton (ed.),
In Six Days: Why Fifty Scientists Choose to Believe in Creation,
Sydney, New Holland, 1999, p.268

So I conclude that Evangelicals who want to hold to evolution as the unbeliever holds to it, and get over the difficulties by saying that Genesis is to be interpreted as poetry or myth and not in a factual manner, cannot, in my view, be honest interpreters.

Dr E J Young, *In the Beginning*, Edinburgh,
The Banner of Truth Trust, 1976, p.19

V

The Bible is to be Trusted from Cover to Cover

What the Bible, the Word of God, teaches is absolutely opposed to what we are taught today about evolution on radio, TV, in books, in schools, colleges, universities and by many Christian teachers. Evolution is a religion and the Bible always gives answers to false teaching and religion. Evolutionists are very dogmatic in their views; statements such as 'The Earth is 12 billion years old' and 'we have evolved from apes' are made with no scientific evidence to back them up. They are told as if they are fact. Andrew Marr, chairing a radio programme on evolution, made this bombastic statement: 'This is the theory we know to be true.'[1]

Creation: how did God do it?

God created by command. 'Let there be', translated from the Hebrew in Genesis 1, is a command – fiat. Time and time again God tells us He did it by command, in Psalm 148:5 and Psalm 33:9, to quote just two of many references. All God had in His mind He brought into being by the power of His Word.

He created by His power, the prophet Jeremiah declares (10:12). God used His Word, we are told in 2 Peter 3:5 and Psalm 33:6–9. God used His wisdom, we read in Psalm 104:24 and Proverbs 8:22–31. It was no accident like the Big Bang, it was His deliberate act, wrote the Apostle Paul (Romans 9:19–24).

The miracles of Jesus – calming the storm, healing, turning water into wine – are all signs He was the creator God. Only He could control all the elements, molecules, atoms that make up our world. He did not need chemicals. Before creation there was nothing. There were no chemicals from which an accidental explosion could take place!

Why did God create?

He did it for and by His son, the Lord Jesus Christ. The earliest creed of the Christian Church makes it very clear. 'He is the image of the invisible God, the firstborn over all creation. For by him all things were created: things in heaven and on earth, visible and invisible, whether thrones or powers or rulers or authorities; *all things were created by him and for him*. He is before all things, and in him all things hold together. And he is the head of the body, the church; he is the beginning and the firstborn from among the dead, so that in everything he might have the supremacy' (Colossians 1:15–18). One day Jesus will return to claim His rightful inheritance.

What does the Bible text teach about creation? (read Genesis 1:1 to 2:3)

The Hebrew text clearly indicates that the day mentioned in Genesis 1 is intended to denote a twenty-four-hour period. Notice each creative act ends with, 'The evening and the morning were the ... day,' etc. Hebrew scholars agree that 'twenty-four-hour day' conveys the meaning of the text. The Hebrew '*yom*', meaning day, is used in Genesis chapter 1, and to underline the nature of the day, the phrase, 'The evening and the morning were...' is added after each creative day. It is interesting to note how the word '*yom*' is used in the Book of Genesis. This valuable information is in *The Answers Book*:

- Outside Genesis I, *yom* is used with a number 410 times and each time it means an ordinary day – why would Genesis 1 be the exception?
- Outside Genesis I, *yom* is used with the word 'evening' or 'morning' 23 times. 'Evening' and 'morning' appear in association, but without *yom*, 38 times. All 61 times the text refers to an ordinary day – why would Genesis 1 be the exception?
- In Genesis 1:5, *yom* occurs in context with the word 'night'. Outside of Genesis 1, 'night' is used with *yom* 53 times – each time it means an ordinary day. Why would Genesis 1 be the exception?[2]

Why do many Christians want to treat Genesis chapter 1 differently? The only answer can be that they want the days of Genesis

1 to be billions or millions of years to accommodate the long-age theories of evolutionary thinking. Unless we accept that the days of creation in Genesis are twenty-four-hour days, it makes a mockery in understanding the text of Exodus 20:9–11: 'Six days you shall labour and do all your work, but the seventh day is a Sabbath to the Lord your God. On it you shall not do any work, neither you, nor your son or daughter, nor your manservant or maidservant, nor your animals, nor the alien within your gates. For in six days the Lord made the heavens and the earth, the sea, and all that in them, but he rested on the seventh day.'

Dr James Barr, Regis Professor of Hebrew, Oxford University, made this statement:

> So far as I know, there is no professor of Hebrew or Old Testament at any world-class university who does not believe that the writer(s) of Genesis 1–11 intended to convey to their readers the ideas (a) creation took place in a series of six days which were the same as the days of 24 hours we now experience (b) the figures contained in the Genesis genealogies provided by simple addition a chronology from the beginning of the world up to later stages in the biblical story (c) Noah's Flood was understood to be world-wide and extinguish all human and animal life except for those in the ark.[3]

Professor Marcus Dods, New College, Edinburgh, states:

> If, for example, the word 'day' in these chapters [Genesis 1 and 2] does not mean a period of twenty-four hours, the interpretation of Scripture is hopeless.[4]

Air Commodore P J Wiseman, an authority on Middle Eastern antiquities, writes, 'I suggest that every time the days are mentioned in both these passages [Genesis chapters 1 and 2] they are intended to be taken literally as ordinary days.'[5]

These views are little known to many Christians and it is for that reason they are given in this book. It is the author's aim to challenge our thinking and to set the reader to seek the answers to searching questions.

Compare the Bible's order of creation with that of the evolutionists. The biblical text teaches an order of creation that conflicts with man's evolutionary theories which they believe have backing of scientific evidence:

COMPARE GOD'S ACCOUNT OF CREATION WITH THAT OF EVOLUTION

Book of Genesis:	Evolution:
Thousands of years ago. By command of God. Planned by God. Created in twenty-four-hour days.	Billions of years ago. Big Bang. By accident – no originator. All life evolved over time.
Genesis chapters one and two written by God.	Unproven theories of men.
Verses 1–5. Day one: Earth/heavens (space),* light/darkness. Read: 2 Corinthians 4:6 & Hebrews 1:10.	Stars and sun, Earth molten blob.
Verses 6–8. Day two: Separated waters. Atmosphere/sky. Verses 9–13. Day three: Seas, dry land, plant life in abundance. Verses 14–19. Day four: Greater and lesser light (sun/moon) and stars. Verses 20–23. Day five: Birds and sea creatures.	The Cassini-Huygens Mission to Saturn (June 2004), sent back images of a water geyser on Enceladus, one of its 62 moons. Deep Impact, a NASA experiment July 2005; spacecraft impacts comet Temple 1. Astronomers observed by spectrum analysis compounds that only form in water. The Apostle Peter wrote: 'the earth was formed out of water and by water'. 2 Peter 3:5
	Whales evolved from land animals.
Verses 24–31. Day six: Two separate acts of creation: land animals and Adam.	Dinosaurs extinct millions of years before man evolved from Hominids.
Chapter 2, verses 1–2. Day seven: Blessed by God and set aside – made holy. God ceased his creative work.	Day of rest and worship not kept. Evolution is progressing through billions of years.
No disease, death – perfection – 'very good'. Man the centre of God's creation. God's plan of salvation. The fall of Adam. Regenerate man lives for ever with God.	Billions of years of accidents and death. Life with no purpose or hope, leading to crime and violence. Oblivion!

*Notice in verse 1, 'the heavens and the earth' – there is no Hebrew word for universe. In Scripture God always speaks of Himself 'filling the heavens and the earth' (see Genesis 14:19; Jeremiah 23:24; Genesis 14:22; 2 Kings 19:15; Psalms 115:15, etc.). Verse 3: God did not create light, God is light (1 John 1:5). The Bible states that in God's new creation there will be no need of the sun (Revelation 21:23 and 22:5). On day four God made the sun, moon and stars to serve their particular functions without which the Earth would be unfit for human habitation. From day four, it could only be a solar day; no other interpretation is possible. After every creation act except one, God said it was good. In verses 6–8, God separated the water 'from under the expanse to the water above it.' This canopy of water in the upper atmosphere was to be used by God to deluge the Earth, in judgement upon man, but Noah and his family were saved. Genesis chapters 1–11 are a sure foundation for all sixty-six books of the Bible.

I repeat, there was light before the sun was energised – God does not need the sun for His existence or to gauge time, we need the sun for our physical existence. That is why God made man and animals last, on the sixth day. The Bible teaches man did not evolve from animals or for that matter from sea creatures or birds as taught by David Attenborough on his TV series. It is not possible for man to evolve. For example, man's knee joint cannot evolve, as it is irreducible. The failure or underdevelopment of any part makes the knee useless, as you will agree if you have ever suffered from a torn cartilage or some other damage. Man had to be fully developed to survive on his own. Notice, every time God created, He thought it was good. There was no death or suffering. Chapter 2 of Genesis gives us an insight into the perfect creation God made; it enlarges on chapter 1. In chapter 2 we are told that woman was made out of man's body and in verse 24 we are told this is why the only foundation for marriage is between one man and one woman.

A biblical genealogy of man

Genesis chapters 4 to 11 record the unbroken genealogy down to Abraham, a period of nearly 2,200 years from the creation of

Adam, including the worldwide flood and the tower of Babel. There is a period of about 2,000 years from Abraham to Christ and, as we know, 2,000 years since His birth: total about 6,200 years! About how far back did creation take place? Many people think that man could not have been created several thousands of years ago, although the Bible, the infallible Word of God, gives all the genealogical family tree from Adam, ample evidence of a *young Earth*. Who should we believe: atheistic evolutionists with their hundreds of thousands and billions, or the Bible, the Word of God?

Chapter 3 tells us about man's fall, the cause and result of sin, and explains that at that point death entered into the world. No animal died until Adam sinned (3:21). No animal was killed for food by Adam. Genesis 1:29–30 tells us that only vegetable matter was eaten. It was not until after the flood that God gave permission for animals to be eaten (9:3). The Apostle Paul teaches in Romans 5 that death reigned from Adam, because of his sin, but Jesus, a 'sinless second Adam', was God's atoning sacrifice for sin. Jesus and the Apostles believed in a real man, Adam.

Notes

[1] *Start the Week*, BBC Radio 4, 9 February 2009
[2] Ken Ham, Jonathan Sarfati and Carl Wieland, *The Answers Book*, ed. by Don Batten, Answers in Genesis, 1999, p.26
[3] Dr James Barr, Regius Professor at Oxford University, letter to David C C Watson, 23 April 1984, quoted in *The Answers Book*, p.27
[4] Professor Marcus Dods, *Expositor's Bible*, Edinburgh, T & T Clark, p.4 as cited by D F Kelly, *Creation and Change*, Fearn, Ross-shire, Christian Focus Publications, 1997, p.50 and quoted in *The Answers Book*, p.27
[5] Air Commodore P J Wiseman, *Creation Revealed in Six Days*, London, Marshall Morgan & Scott, 1949, p.18

Quotable Quotes

The real issue before the Church today, and for that matter before every individual Christian, is whether the Bible is any longer to be regarded and accepted as a trustworthy teacher of doctrine. In other words, when the Bible testifies as to its own nature, are we to pay heed to what it has to say? When the Bible tells us clearly what kind of a Book it is, are we to reject its testimony as unworthy of belief? That is the real issue which faces us today.

It is necessary to give due heed to the seriousness of this issue. Hitherto the Church has derived all her doctrines from the Scriptures. Whenever in the course of her long history the question arose, What is to be believed? it was to the Bible that the Church turned. To frame an answer to the question, What is God? the Church did not turn to her greatest minds, but to the Bible. Again, to settle the question of how many persons there are in the Godhead, the Church went to the Bible to find an answer. Who is Jesus Christ? What must I do to be saved? Who is the Holy Spirit? Is Jesus Christ the only Saviour and Redeemer? For the answers to these and to a thousand other questions, answers which have found formulation in her great creeds, the Church has listened to the words of the Bible. In fact, the creeds are nothing more than attempts upon the part of man to formulate accurately what it was believed the Bible taught. How much loving and devoted labour has gone into the writing of these creeds! How much care and precision has been exercised in their composition! The reason for such loving devotion is to be found simply in the fact that the authors of the creeds were striving to the best of their ability to set forth what they believed the teaching of the Bible to be. Until the present day the Church has exercised great toil and care in an endeavour to present to the world her message, a message which she firmly believed was derived from the Sacred Scriptures themselves.

Professor E J Young, *Thy Word is Truth*, Edinburgh,
Banner of Truth Trust, 1963, pp.28–29

When we speak of the canon of Scripture, the word 'canon' has a simple meaning, It means the list of books contained in Scripture, the list of books recognised as worthy to be included in the sacred writings of a worshipping community ... Before the word 'canon' came to be used in the sense of 'list', it was used in another sense by the Church – in the phrase 'the rule of faith' or 'the rule of truth'. In the earlier Christian centuries this was a summary of Christian teaching, believed to reproduce what the apostles themselves taught, by which any system of doctrine offered for Christian acceptance, or any interpretation of biblical writings, was to be assessed. But when once the limits of Holy Scripture came to be generally agreed upon, Holy Scripture itself came to be regarded as the rule of faith.

F F Bruce, *The Canon of Scripture*, Glasgow,
Chapter House, 1988, pp.17–18

VI

How the Biblical Records of Creation Came Down to Us

We know how precise and accurate the Scribes were in copying one document from another. Any mistake meant the copy had to be destroyed. Jesus alludes to this in Matthew 5:18 (*Authorised Version*): 'Till heaven and earth pass [away], one jot or one tittle shall in no wise pass from the law, till all be fulfilled.' The jot and tittle are the smallest vowel/letter pointings in the Hebrew script. We also know that the Egyptians and Assyrians had their methods of recording events before the invention of parchment made from skins and papyri. These are records on stone or baked clay, the most durable of all writing materials (compare this with paper; don't try to use your floppy disc as a teapot stand), that are thousands of years old. Examples are in our museums telling of creation and a flood. But these accounts are very different from the Genesis record. Genesis is only one of two monotheistic accounts of creation. More about the other later.

During my career in international trade finance I remember being shown a copy of a prism giving details of a banking transaction (called forfeiting) over 4,000 years old. It was to buy a field of cereal that a farmer had sown and when it was ripe there was a guarantee that the farmer would part with it in consideration for the money he had already received. It is estimated that there are over half a million records on baked clay recovered from excavations now in museums. Messages and public records were almost as common as paper is today, 4,000 years ago. Pictographic writing has been traced back to civilisations of 3500 BC. We still use this method of conveying messages, on our highways, on safety signs and for many other uses.

P J Wiseman, in his book *Creation Revealed in Six Days* (1948), sets out to prove that Genesis 1 and 2:1–4 is a very ancient document written originally on stone, and the six twenty-four-hour days constitute the duration of time it took the scribe to record on stone each of the creative acts of God as dictated by God, not the time that it took God to do His work of creation.[1] However, although Wiseman's work on cuneiform antiquities is to be applauded, there is no biblical evidence to support his view about the recording by scribes of the creation account. If the scribe worked on clay as did the Assyrians, then the record of each of God's creative acts would hardly have taken a full day to write and could have been continued at any time, provided the clay was kept moist.

Furthermore there are no Hebrew scholars to my knowledge who have studied the text and hold similar views to Wiseman. In the first chapter of the Book of Genesis the words 'then God said' show God's act of creation was by command. God shows His authority over all matter or brings it into existence from absolutely nothing (*ex nihilo*). God willed His creation into being. The Apostle Paul reminds us that it is God who commands, 'For it is the God who commanded light to shine out of darkness who has shone in our hearts to give light of the knowledge of the glory of God in the face of Jesus Christ' (2 Corinthians 4:6, *Revised Authorised Version*). Jesus showed He was God by His authority over matter when He stilled the storm or fed thousands from a few loaves and fishes.

In his book *Illustrations from Biblical Archaeology*, P J Wiseman's son, Donald J Wiseman, writes, 'Among the traditions of the Sumerian people are several that allude to the introduction of civilisation, the creation of man and of animals, and to the beginnings of the arts and crafts. The most complete version of the Creation Epic has survived on a series of seven, originally six, clay tablets commonly named after the opening words *Enuma elish*, "when on high".'[2] According to many scholars, these narratives borrow heavily from the much earlier Bible's Book of Genesis. *The Early Writing of Genesis* by Dr Bill Cooper (CSM Pamphlet No. 377) is a helpful work on this subject and has some very interesting pictures of early seals.

Wiseman compares the Genesis creation record with similar tablets from Babylon which ended with a colophon. A 'colophon' is like the title page in a modern book.

THE CHART BELOW SHOWS THE INTRODUCTION TO THE
SECOND CHAPTER OF THE BOOK OF GENESIS IF IT HAD
ORIGINATED IN BABYLON

(However, the author will show that the Biblical record of
creation pre-dates Babylon)

Babylon colophon gave this information:	Compare: Genesis 1–2:1–4, to a Babylonian title page
Title of document:	'The heavens and the earth'
Date of writing:	'In the day that the Lord God created the earth and heavens'
Serial number of tablet in series:	It was written on a series of tablets (numbered one to six) – Genesis 1
Statement if it finished the series:	It states after the sixth tablet that the writing was finished (God rested on the seventh day)
The name of scribe:	The only name appearing on this colophon is God

Note: The 'title' given to an ancient piece of writing was usually taken
from the opening words of the first tablet. In this instance the title is 'The
heavens and the earth'.

Who compiled the Patriarchal records? Some people say that the
story of creation and the flood as well as the biographies of the
Patriarchs were handed down by word of mouth. However, if
these records were verbal, then the Bible accounts would not be
in the amazing detail, style and clarity in which we have them
today. The accounts of creation and Noah's flood would be very
much like those hundreds of myth-like accounts we have from
other cultures.

Some writings in circulation at the time of Jesus' ministry
named the scribe of Genesis 1 to 2:4 as Enoch (the man whom

God took body and soul, without him experiencing death as we know it (Hebrews 11:5)). Enoch was a contemporary of Adam and Eve, Seth, Enos, Cainan, Mahelaleel and Jared. Enoch could have received the account of creation from any of these relatives. Some Bible students believe that Adam, an intelligent man, may have been the scribe used by God before he sinned. We will look at Adam in another chapter. God may have written the creation account with His own 'finger'. In Deuteronomy 9:10 it is recorded that God wrote the tables of the covenant with His 'finger'. Copies of these documents were kept in the Ark of the Covenant. Jesus wrote in the sand with His finger when confronted with the woman taken in adultery and her accusers, showing His divinity.

Dr E F Kevan, Principal of the London Bible College, in his commentary on Genesis states:

> There is the amazing likelihood, however, that Moses may have possessed original writings, possibly on clay tablets, and that these may have come from the hands of men like Noah, Shem, Terah and others. That this is anything more than a possibility it would be foolish to assert, but it is a theory that is not without some reasonable justification.[3]

In his book *The Genesis Record*, Dr Morris suggests that:

> These records were kept, possibly on tablets of stone, in such a way that they would be preserved until they finally came into Moses' possession. He then selected those that were relevant to his own purpose (as guided by the Holy Spirit) ... It is probable that these original documents can still be recognised by the key phrase: These are the generations of ... there are eleven of these divisions marked off in Genesis.[4]

GENEALOGICAL RECORD: ADAM TO JACOB

Book of Genesis	Details of Each Division
Chapters 2, verse 4	This is the account of the creation of the heavens, earth and man.
Chapter 5, verse 1	This is the book of the genealogy of Adam's line.
Chapter 6, verse 9	This is the genealogy of Noah.
Chapter 10, verse 1	These is the genealogy of the sons of Noah: Shem, Ham and Japheth.
Chapter 11, verse 10	This is the genealogy of Shem.
Chapter 11, verse 27	This is the genealogy of Terah.
Chapter 25, verse 12	This is the genealogy of Ishmael, Abraham and Hagar's son.
Chapter 25, verse 19	This is the genealogy of Isaac, Abraham and Sarah's son.
Chapter 36, verse 1	This is the genealogy of Esau, who is Edom.
Chapter 36, verse 9	This is the genealogy of Esau's sons (the father of the Edomites in Mt Seir).
Chapter 37, verse 2	This is the genealogy of Jacob.

Note: Remember, chapter and verses are not in the original text but added for us centuries later. Chapter 5, verse 1 states the genealogy was written down.

Each of the eleven sections points to the narrative already recorded and indicates the scribe or owner of the tablet or record. Anyone who has been involved in tracing their ancestors would have been grateful if family information had been kept in this orderly way in more recent times. Each division is just like a family album, a snapshot, with more detailed histories of Abraham, Isaac and Jacob than for the others, with the exception of Noah, who went through dramatic events that changed our planet. Do you know Noah's father, Lamech, was a contemporary of Adam? Noah missed meeting Adam by 126 years!

We can see the wonders of creation (Romans 1:20), but unless we had the Genesis record we could never know accurately the events of creation week. God would not in His wisdom leave the creation account to become corrupted by it being passed by word of mouth until Moses could write it down, some 3,000 years after the event. Many of the great Hebrew scholars believe that the prose of Genesis 1 has been preserved from the most ancient of times. If it had been written later by Moses, then he would have used the Hebrew words for sun, moon and the Sabbath day. The words used in the original text speak of lesser and greater light and the seventh day. What an amazing story that God should let us know the facts of creation and give us a family tree from the first man, Adam, to Jesus of Nazareth, by ensuring the preservation of these accounts, some part perhaps written by Earth's earliest inhabitant!

Reasons Genesis should be taken as credible history

Many people suggest there are no records of Abraham or the events that his nation went through, and that he was not a real historical figure. However, the Old Testament is a book about the history of God's chosen people. Jewish people all over the world have accepted it as the history of their nation. The Venerable Bede wrote the history of the early years of Britain, but no one asks for this account to be proved by the existence of other writings. Why should the Old Testament be any less reliable on the history of the Jewish nation than Bede's work on the English?

Genesis is a history book. Miss Childs, my history teacher, would have been very angry with me if I had not taken the period of AD 1485–1763 covered by my textbook literally or if I had thought it was a book of poetry. Heaven help me if I had said, 'Some of it's a fable.' She was, however, a good teacher of history and I was convinced it was fact! Anyway, there was plenty of evidence that it all happened. I learnt that about 500 years ago Henry VIII had six wives. There is far more evidence for 'special creation'. It was from her that I first learnt about the great religious awakenings of the Reformation and eighteenth-century revival. I was blessed indeed to have a Christian teacher. We are blessed that God teaches us through His book, the Bible, whose authenticity and inspiration are without doubt.

How does God feel about us not believing the truth? He created everything and, as He was there, He put facts in the Book of Genesis so we should know the truth. God must be angry with the Church, which has allowed itself to be deceived by atheistic evolutionists who do not believe chapters 1–11 are factual. The books of the Bible are a variety of writings, including poetry and apocalyptic writings, and must be read accordingly. Those history books of the Bible must be read as history.

Jesus, on eleven occasions, is recorded as quoting the flood and creation accounts as being actual events that took place. The Apostles refer to Adam as a historic person. There are over 100 references in the NT to Genesis chapters 1–11. If Adam never lived, then it makes a laughing stock of all the Bible. Would Jesus, who, being God, took on the form of a man, quote fables as fact? Scripture always makes it clear when Jesus was teaching by parables.

God's promise to the Chinese

This is the title of a book by Ethel Nelson, Richard Broadberry and Ginger Tong Chock. Richard Broadberry is a Transfusion Medicine Research Scientist. When we spoke he confirmed that the book is the result of researching thousands of oracle bone specimens. These writings, found in China, which record the offering of bull sacrifices to 'ShangDi' (pronounced like Shaddai, the name for God in the Old Testament) way back to the time of Emperor Shun (c. 2230 BC – before Abraham). From a very early date the Chinese were making offerings to 'ShangDi' on top of Mount Tai in Shan-Dong. Much later the practice was trans-ferred to the Altar and Temple of Heaven in Beijing, which today are tourist attractions. These sacrifices ceased in the sixteenth century AD. The people who invented the original characters inscribed them on tortoise plastron and ox bones. They must have known and believed in an identical account of creation and the Earth's beginnings as recorded in the Book of Genesis. The authors state:

Historically, the Shang Dynasty's (1766–1122 BC) recognition of ShangDi as the true Supreme God over all gods may have continued into the Zhou Dynasty (1122–255 BC), but by the Han Dynasty (206 BC–AD 24), ShangDi was largely forgotten. Buddhism and Taoism, in addition to the interwoven religion of ancestor-worship, predominated. However, all traces and knowledge of the original God of China have not been erased. We believe a beautiful history of the beginnings of the human race on the newly created planet earth have been perfectly preserved in the ancient character-writing of the Chinese language. The written language was invented simultaneously with the development of early Chinese culture.[5]

The Oracles all tell of God who created by command, and had fellowship with Adam and Eve who were tempted by a serpent and sinned. If you intend to take a trip to China read the book first.

The Old Testament history of the Jewish nation is reliable

The argument that is often thrown at the historicity of the Old Testament is that there is no evidence that confirms that the Israelites ever went into Egypt or that 400 years later they made an exodus.

In the 1950s a Russian Jew, Immanuel Velikovsky, wrote a series of books, *Ages in Chaos*. In volume 1 (from the Exodus to King Akhnaton) he set about to explain that the great epics of the Old Testament, such as the exodus of the Israelites from Egypt, the plagues, and Joshua's long day, were corroborated by the histories of many other civilisations, such as the Mayans, Aztecs, Greeks, Finns, Chinese and Egyptians. He found that these civilisations had reported the water turning to blood, darkness when it should have been day, a long day (or long night) and other global phenomena. He went on to explain why he believed his research proved that the plagues and the exodus had left Egypt open to the invasion of the Hyksos. He also argues very convincingly that the Egyptian queen Hatshepsut is the Queen of Sheba who visited King Solomon as recorded in the Old Testament

(1 Kings:10 and 11). Velikovsky quotes from Scripture and also from 'Leiden 344', written by an ancient Egyptian named Ipuwer. He relies on the translation of Professor Alan Gardner. Many other researchers have written similar views rejecting criticism of Old Testament history, and some of these are mentioned in the select bibliography. Velikovsky's research was applauded by Albert Einstein and Professor H H Hess, although they did not always share his views.

The *Al-Ahram* daily newspaper has recently carried a dispatch reporting the discovery of ancient coins in unsorted items in the Museum of Egypt vaults.[6] It was reported that the researcher found coins with Joseph's name in hieroglyphs. There are also images of a man and a cow on the coins. The biblical story of Joseph can be found in Genesis 37–50.

Notes

[1] Wiseman, *Creation Revealed in Six Days*

[2] Donald J Wiseman, *Illustrations from Biblical Archaeology*, London, The Tynedale Press, 1958, p.7

[3] Kevan, *The New Bible Commentary*, p.75

[4] Dr Henry M Morris, *The Genesis Record*, Grand Rapids MI, Baker Book House Co., 1998, pp.26–27

[5] Ethel Nelson, Richard Broadberry and Ginger Tong Chock, *God's Promise to the Chinese*, Dunlap TN, Read Books Publisher, 1997, pp.9–10

[6] http://www.memri.org/bin/articles.cgi?Page=archives&Area=sd&ID=SP256109

Quotable Quotes

Can a man be both a scientist and a Christian? Is there a conflict between science and the Scriptures? Why do some scientists believe in God and yet others reject Him? Anyone can write a question mark over anything, and some people with a scientific turn of mind seem to take delight in writing a question mark over the Bible and God, shocking and shaking people who have held a faith in God in their hearts. Each of us has built within us a capacity for doubt, and a capacity for faith, with the will of man being the determining factor. Why does one scientist, in possession of the same facts as another, believe and accept Jesus Christ and the teachings of the Bible, and the other reject Him? Since they are both scientists, it couldn't be the facts of science that keep the one from believing. No, it is simply that he exercises his will to doubt rather than to believe. Faith or doubt are determined by the will, not by proof and facts. The believer has everything to gain and nothing to lose.

Dr Edward F Blick, *A Scientific Analysis of Genesis*, Oklahoma, Hearthstone Publishing, 1991, p.1

While the quest for understanding continues, we need to recognise that our current 'scientific' track record is disturbingly bleak. If you examine the continuing articles in the vanguard of the 'new sciences', it is humbling to recognise how much of our current ontological understanding of the nature of our universe are elaborate extrapolations built on disturbingly small glimpses of actual data. It appears that many investigators consistently draw vast conclusions from half-vast information!

Chuck Missler, *Personal Update*, Waterlooville, Koinonia House Europe, 2005, vol. 15, no. 2

THREE OF THE JEWISH PRINCIPLES OF FAITH

6. I believe with perfect faith that all the words of the prophets are true.

7. I believe with perfect faith that the prophecy of Moses our teacher, peace be unto him, was true, and that he was the chief of prophets, both of those that preceded and of those that follow him.

8. I believe with perfect faith that the whole Law, now in our possession, is the same that was given to Moses our teacher, peace unto him.

Extracted from the Thirteen Principles of Faith, from the Daily Prayer Book of the United Hebrew Congregations of the British Empire (1935 Edition). These Articles of the Jewish Creed were formulated by Moses Maimonides in the twelfth century

Genesis, of course, had always been understood as standing in a special place, starting as it does with the God-given accounts both of the Creation and the Fall of Man – both of them the very foundation of theology. Moreover, as the first book in the world (as it was thought to be), by the world's first author, Moses, it can express something important about Scripture, that is, about religion with a book at the heart.

David Daniell, *William Tyndale, a Biography*,
Yale University Press, 2001, pp.287–8

VII

The Theory of Evolution Flies in the Face of Scientific Facts

Deoxyribonucleic Acid (DNA)

> The body's most precious substance is stored deep inside the cells, in the tiny nucleus, namely the genetic information, known as the genome. If this information were to be written down using the alphabet, it would fill one thousand books, each having 1,000 pages with 3,000 letters to the page. The human genome (inherited material) consists of three thousand million genetic 'letters'. If all these letters were typed in one line, it would extend from the North Pole to the equator.
>
> Werner Gitt[1]

The human DNA has over 3 billion nucleotides. The information, fully sequenced, would fill the equivalent of 1,000 large encyclopaedias. Human and chimpanzee DNA similarity is often claimed as evidence that humans evolved from apes. However, it will be shown in the next section that this is an impossibility and can only point us to a common designer – God.

All cells carry coded instructions called genes for all their functions. Sometimes there are copying mistakes in these instructions that are called mutations. It is frequently taught by evolutionists that, over millions of years, mutations produce the necessary information for man's evolutionary process to take place.

However, many scientists acknowledge that the kind of changes we see in living things do not indicate life coming into being by any evolutionary process. Evolution of molecules to man requires new complex genetic information. This can only be

71

likened to *adding* a new software programme to a computer. These changes can never happen by natural selection and mutations, because these only lead to a *loss* of genetic information. If you are unsure as to the validity of the claim that mutations and natural selection cannot produce new information, then read what some scientists and teachers have written:

> Life is built on information. This information is contained in that molecule of heredity, DNA, which makes up the genes of an organism. Therefore, to argue that natural selection and mutations are the basic mechanisms of evolutionary process, one must show that these processes produce the information responsible for the design that is evident in living things ... Natural selection only operates on the information contained in the genes – it does not produce new information. Actually, this is consistent with the Bible's account of origins, in that God created distinct 'kinds' of animals and plants to reproduce after its own kind.
>
> K Ham, *Is There Really a God?*[2]

> To insist, even with Olympian assurance, that life appeared quite by chance and evolved in this fashion, is an unfounded supposition which I believe to be wrong and not in accordance with the facts.
>
> Pierre-Paul Grasse, *Evolution of Living Organisms*[3]

> One must conclude that, contrary to the established and current wisdom, a scenario describing the genesis of life on earth by chance and natural causes which can be accepted on the basis of fact and not faith has not yet been written.
>
> H P Yockey, 'A Calculation of the Probability of Spontaneous Biogenesis by Information Theory'[4]

> When it comes to the origin of life on earth, there are only two possibilities: creation or spontaneous generation (evolution). There is no third way. Spontaneous generation was disproved 100 years ago, but this leads us only to one other conclusion: that of supernatural creation. We cannot accept that on philosophical grounds; therefore we choose to believe the impossible: that life arose spontaneously by chance.
>
> Dr George Wald, Nobel Prize Winner in Science[5]

When all scientists have the same evidence before them, I find it is incredible that there are those who still believe in evolution! Preconceived ideas which have been passed on to us or taught by those who believe in the theory of evolution often blind us to the true interpretation of the evidence. We learnt in the earlier chapters of this book that evolution is a religion founded on a misplaced faith. Jesus and the Apostles call on us to abandon that misplaced faith and to believe in the God of special creation.

The Earth is not permanent and God has said He will create a new heaven and Earth (Revelation 21:1; Mark 13:31; Luke 21:33). There is ample evidence that things are in decline and we deceive ourselves if we believe that a better world is evolving (read Romans 8:18–25). The only real hope for the Christian is in God's promised new creation where all believers will have new bodies. This new creation is graphically illustrated in Revelation chapter 21.

Those fossils and bones

The *Today* programme on BBC Radio 4 reported the discovery of 'Rutland Man': the second supposed discovery in the UK of Neanderthal man, who we are told lived 40,000 years ago. The other was a tooth found in Wales! However, so far no human bones have been found in Rutland, only a few axe heads and animal bones. How gullible we are! Any police authority homicide squad would query the competence of forensic scientists who can make such pronouncements without reference to the corpse!

Civil engineer Malcolm Bowden gave up much of his time to refuting the teaching of evolutionists. He went on to teach that Piltdown Man was a fake. It took the Natural History Museum years to accept the same evidence. Not all discoveries, however, are fakes. But the discovery of human/ape-like skeletons is often open to conflicting interpretations due to an individual's preconceived ideas.

Biologist and orthodontist Dr J Cuozzo has studied the remains of Neanderthal man and you can read about it in his book *Buried Alive*.[6] He has found that these men were buried after being painted with red ochre and with grave jaspers similar to those of the Ubaidians who lived between 3000 and 2500 BC in the Middle East, and whose civilisation gave way to that of the Sumerians. They decorated their caves with paintings showing dinosaurs fighting with mammoths. Dinosaurs were supposed to have died out 65 million years ago, long before mammoths! Dr Cuozzo has come to the conclusion that Neanderthals are humans who lived longer (like the Old Testament Patriarchs) than we do today but matured more slowly, as we would expect with those who lived to a great age before the Earth was changed so radically after Noah's flood. This is ample scientific evidence for the great age of people named in the early chapter of the Book of Genesis.

Dr Cuozzo's research produced some interesting information:

- Some skulls were incorrectly assembled in the museums, giving the impression the skulls were akin to those of apes.

- From medical science we know that our bodies cease growing but our skulls continue to grow very slowly. The bones over the eyes grow larger as we get older to protect the eyes from damage that which would otherwise be caused from the effect of chewing food. This feature was very pronounced in Neanderthals.

- The study of Neanderthals confirms that people who lived longer, like Methuselah, would have developed more slowly. Note in the Book of Genesis the age when they had their first born was between the ages of 65 and 187. Analysis of skulls over the centuries points to faster physical development in humans today.

- Neanderthals from the German valley which they are named after lived much nearer to our times than many people wish to believe. They have become the joke of many film-makers. *The Clan of the Cave Bear*, made in 1986, was supposed to depict the life of Neanderthals using their own language, which happily for picture-goers had subtitles in English!

Scientist Dr A J Monty White in his book *Wonderfully Made*, looking at the scientific evidence for the evolution of one life form to another, comes to this conclusion:

> It cannot be over emphasised, however, that the assumed ancestor of apes and humans has never been found and its existence is purely hypothetical, in spite of what is written in popular evolutionary books. The evolutionists cannot even identify our supposed ancestral hominoid [hominid], as the following recent quotation shows: 'Candidates for intermediate ancestors that have been proposed include two from Kenya known as *Proconsul* and *Kenyapithecus*; two from India, Pakistan, China and Kenya called *Ramapithecus* and *Sivapithecus*; and two from Europe called *Rudapithecus* and *Dryopithecus* ... Despite much debate and speculation, none of these primates has been finally accepted as a human progenitor.' In other words, there is no transitional form linking humans with an animal ancestor. No more really needs to be said! There is no evidence from the fossil record linking humans to their supposed animal ancestors.[7]

The absence of intermediary fossils is of great concern to evolutionists

> The absence of fossil evidence for intermediary stages between major transitions in organic design, indeed our inability, even in our imagination, to construct functional intermediates in many cases, has been a persistent and nagging problem for gradualistic accounts of evolution.
>
> Stephen Jay Gould, Professor of Geology and Palaeontology[8]

> Despite the bright promise that palaeontology provides a means of 'seeing' evolution, it has presented some nasty difficulties for evolutionists, the most notorious of which is the presence of 'gaps' in the fossil record. Evolution requires intermediate forms between species and palaeontology does not provide them. The gaps must therefore be a contingent feature of the record.
>
> David B Kitts, PhD, School of Geology and Geophysics, University of Oklahoma[9]

For 150 years since Darwin published his theory, millions of fossils have been dug up and no evidence has been found that, through an evolutionary process, one species has developed into another quite distinct species. It is the faith of the evolutionist that keeps them digging in the vain hope that some day their diligent search may reward them.

Notes

[1] Werner Gitt, *The Wonder of Man*, Bielefeld, Christliche Literature-Verbreitung, 2003, p.75

[2] Ken Ham, *Is There Really a God?*, Florence KY, USA, Answers in Genesis, 1998, pp.11–12

[3] Pierre-Paul Grasse, *Evolution of Living Organisms*, Academic Press, New York, 1977, p.107, quoted in *The Revised Quote Book*, p.21

[4] H P Yockey, 'A Calculation of the Probability of Spontaneous Biogenesis by Information Theory', *Journal of Theoretical Biology*, vol. 67, 1977, p.396, quoted in *The Revised Quote Book*, p.3

[5] As cited by Dr Stanley Swinney, *Confessions of a Rocket Scientist*, Greeley, Colorado, Chambers College Press, 2005, p.78

[6] Dr Jack Cuozzo, *Buried Alive: The Startling Truth about Neanderthal Man*, Green Forest AR, Master Books, 1998

[7] Dr A J Monty White, *Wonderfully Made*, Durham, Evangelical Press, 1989, p.40, contains quote from K F Weaver, 'Search for our Ancestors', *National Geographic*, 1985, pp.560–623

[8] Stephen Jay Gould, 'Is a New General Theory of Evolution Emerging?', *Paleobiology*, vol. 6, 1980, p.127 quoted in *The Revised Quote Book*, p.8

[9] David B Kitts, 'Palaeontology and Evolutionary Theory', *Evolution*, vol. 28, 1974, p.467 quoted in *The Revised Quote Book*, p.9

Quotable Quotes

The Mosaic account of the creation is so intimately connected with that of the Deluge that I must ask my young reader (whom alone I presume to address on this subject) to turn to the first chapter of Genesis, and refer to a few verses with me. We soon find a remarkable fact, which shows to my mind that the knowledge of Moses was superhuman...

> Robert Fitzroy's reference to Noah's flood in his *Narrative of the Surveying Voyages of the HMS* Adventure *and* Beagle Appendix 2, Charles Darwin, *Voyage of the* Beagle, London, Penguin Classics, 1989, p.403

How old is the earth? Does it really matter how old it is? How does the answer to this question affect you and your family and even your friends? The answer to this last question is obvious when we consider origins, for there are two irreconcilable views regarding the beginnings of things: evolution and creation. Which one is correct? One thing is certain: if the earth is only a few thousand years old, then evolution cannot be correct, for evolution needs lots of time. This factor cannot be over emphasised for we are told that chance natural processes need to operate over eons of time in order to bring about the evolution of life on earth.

> Dr A J Monty White, *How Old is the Earth?*, Darlington, Evangelical Press, 1985, p.13

Many intelligent people are thoroughly convinced that science has proven the earth to be billions of years old. How can they be wrong? The misconception builds on a neglect of the basic nature of 'science' and a natural desire for moral autonomy. Actually, the age of the earth can be neither proved nor disproved by science. Scientific evidence can be compiled to support one model of earth history as compared to another, but such work amounts to a feasibility study, not proof.

> Dr Jeremy L Walter, quoted in John F Ashton (ed.), *In Six Days, Why Fifty Scientists Choose to Believe in Creation*, Sydney, New Holland Publishers, 1999, pp.2–3

According to the 'Big Bang' theory, the universe began about 10 to 20 billion years ago as an inconceivably small volume of space and matter/energy which has been expanding ever since. However, we are entitled to ask the question: what went bang? In simple terms, 'Nothing can't go bang'. A related question is: when did natural laws governing the physical world come into being? Are we to believe that these laws also are the product of chance? Professor Werner Gitt has recently reviewed the Big Bang theory and notes that, 'many discoveries in recent years with improved instruments and improved observational methods have repeatedly shaken this theory.'

Dr Stephen Taylor, quoted in John F Ashton (ed.),
In Six Days, Why Fifty Scientists Choose to Believe in Creation,
Sydney, New Holland Publishers, 1999, p.285

VIII

Age Concern!

Can we be sure how old the Earth is? Are dating methods reliable? Even scientists tell us otherwise. Some scientists give their views:

> The age of our globe is presently thought to be some 4.5 billion years, based on radiodecay rates of uranium and thorium. Such 'confirmation' may be short-lived, as nature is not to be discovered quite so easily. There has been in recent years the horrible realisation that radiodecay rates are not as constant as previously thought, nor are they immune to environmental influences.
>
> And this could mean that the atomic clocks are reset during some global disaster, and events which brought the Mesozoic to a close may not be 65 million years ago but, rather, within the memory of man.
>
> Frederic B Jueneman[1]

> It is obvious that radiometric techniques may not be the absolute dating methods that they are claimed to be. Age estimates on a given geological stratum by different radiometric methods are often quite different (sometimes by hundreds of millions of years). There is no absolutely reliable long-term radiological 'clock'. The uncertainties inherent in radiometric dating are disturbing to geologists and evolutionists...
>
> William D Stansfield PhD[2]

> However, we do know Someone who was present when all the earth's rocks formed – the Creator Himself. He has told us when that was, in His eye-witness account in the Bible's first book, Genesis, so we know how old all the rocks are. How much better to place our confidence in the Creator who made and knows everything, and who never fails or tells lies, than in a radioactive dating method that has been repeatedly demonstrated to fail and yield false ages for the earth's rocks.
>
> Andrew Snelling, BSc (Hons), PhD (Geology)[3]

Einstein's relativity theories have been telling the world for decades that time is not a constant. Two things are believed (with experimental support) to distort time in relativity theory – one is speed and the other is gravity. Einstein's general theory of relativity, the best theory of gravity we have at present, indicates that **gravity distorts time**.

Quoted from The Answers Book[4]

It is more than probable that God created the universe, the Earth and all on it, so that it was at various stages of development. At creation there would have been stars, plants, birds, fish, animals etc., at all their various stages of growth. If God had not created a 'complete package' Adam would have died from starvation. Similarly this could account for the time light takes to reach our earth from stars. Some have criticised this explanation as showing a deceitful God. It is only deceitful in the eyes of evolutionists because it does not fit their theories. If some plants were not fully developed and fruiting or carrying seed, Adam would have been a dead man within a few days. How would you like to take possession of a property advertised with 'a mature and well-stocked garden' only to find seedlings! Adam and Eve were placed in a well-stocked garden.

We can learn from recent natural disasters

Many of us remember hearing about the devastation caused by the massive volcanic eruption of Mt St Helens, May 1980. Debris flowed fifteen miles down the North Fork of the Toutle River. Around 3,500 vertical feet of material slid nearly 80,000 feet horizontally! The collapse was followed by a pyroclastic blast that scythed down trees seventeen miles away. Over 200 square miles was covered with molten lava spewed from the depths of our planet. Twenty years later there is evidence of that ecological disaster, but much of the fauna and flora have recovered and scientists believe that it will take only 200 years before forest covers the blast area. This all points to the resilience of God's creation. It was possible for the Earth to recover even from Noah's cataclysmal Earth-encompassing flood. Today there are rock formations and canyons made by the lava flows in a matter of days. If scientists had not witnessed the eruption of this volcano and the result, we might have been led to believe that all this took millions of years! Mt St Helens has taught scientists that great changes in the Earth's surface can take only hours and days, not thousands or millions of years as previously thought. Some scientists believe that the Grand Canyon was gorged out by massive glaciers in a matter of days. We are only just beginning to learn of God's might demonstrated in the power of volcanoes, ice, and water.

> After St Helens, geologists all over the world began to see more clearly the signs of previous volcanic collapse.
>
> *National Geographic*, January 1981

It is not the duration of time (millions of years) that causes the change in the structure of rocks and fossils, but other factors, such as enormous pressures exerted by the Earth and the effect of heat, water and chemicals present. Scientists are able to make diamonds (they can be distinguished by experts from the real thing), opals and coal in a matter of days by recreating the right conditions.

Are dinosaurs millions of years old?

Dr R Plot was the first to find dinosaur bones in 1677. They were thought to be a large elephant. In 1822 Dr M A Mantell found an iguanodon tooth on the Sussex Downs. Today there are about 240 related types. Most of these are represented by a few bones. They are not prehistoric: the Bible teaches that there was no history of death before Adam. No animal or human ever died before Adam sinned. How can we believe there was death when God said 'it was good'? If we believe that there was death before Adam sinned, we go against the teaching of the Bible. Adam lived with dinosaurs. Dinosaurs were made by God with all other animals on day six of creation week. They were created to display God's power and majesty. There is no reason to believe that these peculiar animals did not go on the Ark with Noah. Infant dinosaurs were the size of small sheep. Unfossilised dinosaur bones in Alaska and a T-Rex leg bone containing red blood cells point to the fact that these animals are not millions of years old. *The Sunday Times* (6 August 2000) reported that a well-preserved fossil of an ichthyosaur had been discovered in a Yorkshire quarry. Palaeontologists could tell that its last meal was an extinct sea creature. None of these remains could survive 65 or 225 millions of years in this form. These creatures died very suddenly and were buried by earth, signs of a catastrophic disaster. Death, disease and suffering are the result of the sin of Adam, who lived only thousands of years ago (read Romans 5:12–14 and 1 Corinthians 15:21–22).

Something changed the whole of our planet

Apostle Peter (2 Peter 3:3–6) warns of men who say that 'all things continue as since the creation'. Peter points out that this teaching is false as the environment God created was destroyed by the universal flood (verse 6). The world we live in today is not like the one God created. Because of God's curse on the ground (Genesis 3:17) and the catastrophic flood (Genesis 6–9), these have changed the Earth; and decay has been set in motion. Catastrophism is accepted by an increasing numbers of scientists today even though they may not acknowledge the biblical record.

The Bible teaches that Noah and his family heeded God's warning and they were saved with animals from destruction by placing them (including some dinosaurs) on the Ark, a huge wooden vessel about the size of one of our largest container ships. God saved them from a cataclysmal flood. All the mountains were covered by water, but that was not all! Genesis 7:11 states that all the 'fountains of the deep broke up'. We know that our mountain ranges have been thrown up by huge forces in the Earth's crust. So, before the flood, mountains may have been no more than hills. Water could therefore have covered them completely. This was not just a deluge, but what appears to have been deep volcanic action rupturing the Earth's crust, bringing water, lava, gases and molten rock to the surface, covering all the vegetation which had been already covered with water. Noah and his family were in the safest place! This is the reason we are living on top of a 'post-

Adam/post-flood graveyard' of deposited bones of every possible type. Those who lived before Noah's flood would not recognise the Earth as it is today!

There was no death or suffering until Adam sinned, therefore there are no 'prehistoric' animals. The Apostle Paul wrote, 'Just as sin entered the world through one man, and death through sin, and in this way death came to all men, because all sinned ... death reigned from the time of Adam to the time of Moses, even over those who did not sin by breaking a command, as did Adam, who was a pattern of the one to come' Romans 5:12–14.

Why don't we see dinosaurs today? There are many other animals that have become extinct. Even today conservationists are concerned that many species of animal and insect are near extinction. The forces that caused Noah's flood had a knock-on effect, causing severe climatic and geological changes. Many animals did not survive their new environment. That was the consequence of Adam's sin.

There are about 500 accounts of a universal flood from as many ethnic groups (not races – there is only one race, the descendants of Noah). Only the Bible account is as detailed and stands up to scientific scrutiny. The Ark measured 300 x 50 x 30 cubits (Genesis 6:15), which is 137 x 23 x 13.7 metres (450 x 75 x 45 feet for imperialists!). These are the exact measurements for a large vessel that needed only to be watertight and stable. The dimensions are in exact ratios that are applied when building modern tankers and ocean-going container ships. It didn't need speed as it wasn't on a journey. Only God could provide design and building instructions for a wooden ship that would withstand the tremendous forces unleashed upon it from a year's continuous rain, water and volcanic eruptions. Only a universal flood would have required Noah to build on this scale. According to Ark researchers it would have had the capacity to carry 35,000 animals, and then there was still plenty of room for Noah and family plus food and fodder. I suggest for further details reading *Genesis Flood* by Whitcomb and Morris, or books mentioned in the select bibliography.

Search for the Ark

Many books have been written on this subject. George Hagopian claims to have found, with his uncle, the Ark in a huge glacier on Ararat in 1902 when he was ten years old.[5] During the last years of Imperial Russia, an expedition was reported to have found evidence of the Ark on Ararat, but the files, including photographic evidence, mysteriously disappeared during the Russian Revolution. There have been many attempts to find the Ark, but they have always been abandoned due to the inhospitable weather, human physical exhaustion or the political situation. The Ararat Mountains cover a vast area and reach a height of 5,165 metres. Because of their geographical position they are prone to sudden climatic change, bringing violent electric storms and blizzards at any time of year. Also, a cursory glance at a map will show that this mountain range is in a highly sensitive area straddling the borders of Georgia, Azerbaijan (both formerly part of the Soviet Union), Turkey, Iraq and Iran – no place for your rambling club.

Fernand Navarra tells in his book *The Noah's Ark Expedition* how he made several expeditions to Ararat to search for the Ark.[6] In 1955 he was successful when at about 13,000 feet he found a part of a wooden vessel partially exposed in a glacier. Then, in 1969, returning to the same place, he again found wood by boring through a glacier. Wood samples were studied and considered to be about 5,000 years old.

Dinosaurs are described in the Bible. Actually, you won't find the word 'dinosaur' in the Bible as this word was invented by Sir Richard Owen in 1841: it means 'large lizard'. But descriptions of similar animals are contained in the Bible. Jeremiah (51:34) describes Nebuchadnezzar's action as similar to being swallowed by a dragon. Psalm 74:13–14 describes the head of Leviathan (dragon) being smashed by God. Isaiah (27:1) uses the word 'dragon'. Job (chapters 41 and 42) in graphic detail describes the teeth and rows of scales of a sauropod. The NIV has put the names of animal species in these verses which are not in the original text. The Hebrew text uses the words 'tan' and 'tannin' – dragons. The text names most animals we know but uses 'tan', a general term for dragons, as in Job 30:29, Isaiah 13:22, 34:13 and 43:20, Jeremiah 9:11, 10:22, 14:6, 49:33 and 51:37, Psalm 44:19 and Micah 1:8. 'Tannin' is used in Genesis 1:21 for great sea monsters; in the Authorised King James version this becomes 'whales' and is translated in modern versions as great sea creatures.

Read and substitute dragon or dinosaur and see how they are described in the text of chapters 41 and 42 of the Book of Job. Are the translators in some recent versions of the Bible bowing to evolutionary theories, giving names to these monsters such as elephants, hyenas and jackals? There is evidence in the Bible that dinosaurs lived with men. There is every reason to believe that Adam ate with dinosaurs and Noah slept with them. Today, living on Earth, are animals similar to so-called 'prehistoric animals'. Some fish found as fossils and considered to be millions of years old are alive and well in our oceans, the depths of which have not been fully explored (e.g. coelacanths). Sightings of dinosaur-type creatures have been reported recently from the remote rainforests of Congo and New Guinea!

A decomposing plesiosaur type of mammal was brought to the surface in fishing nets off the coast of New Zealand in 1977. According to the Japanese fisheries-qualified biologist who examined the carcass, there was not the strong ammonia smell of putrefying fish or sharks. Unfortunately the carcass was returned to the sea in order not to contaminate the rest of the catch.

There are other sources from historical reports that tell about dragons. It is so remarkable that throughout the world there are so many stories about dragons. What about St George and the dragon – is it myth, or is there some factual basis for the story? In the Book of Job, chapter 41 is taken up with the description of a most awful beast. I quote verses 18–21:

> His snorting throws out flashes of light; his eyes are like the rays of dawn. Firebrands stream from his mouth; sparks of fire shoot out. Smoke pours from his nostrils as from a boiling pot over a fire of reeds. His breath sets coals ablaze, and flames dart from his mouth.

It is not surprising to read, in a pamphlet written by D Curtis, the following comment on this text from Job:

> Did Dragons really live? That does seem to be borne out by the fossil record. But 'breathing fire'? Surely impossible; until we hear about the exploding Bombardier Beetles roaming Wales. Less than an inch in length, this little creature is endowed with an ability to imitate gunpowder exploding. Hydroquinone and peroxide are made to react by the addition of two enzymes: catalase, which decomposes the peroxide rapidly, and peroxidase, which oxidises the hydroquinones. These enzymes cause the reaction to proceed at an explosive rate (500 bursts a second). The pressure of oxygen gas shoots hot, smelly, bluish vapour of quinones through two nozzles in the back of the insect, quite off-putting to a predator! Could the duck-billed dinosaurs such as the hadrosaurs have had just such a defence mechanism, but in their skulls? These have cavities similar in design to the minute explosion chambers in the Bombardier Beetle. Moreover the skin which, unusually, is fossilised with these dinosaurs appears to have been thick and leathery, and covered with small tubercles.[7]

Notes

[1] Frederic B Jueneman, 'Secular Catastrophism', *Industrial Research and Development*, June 1982, quoted in *The Revised Quote Book*, p.21
[2] William D Stansfield PhD, *The Science of Evolution*, New York, Macmillan, 1997, quoted in *The Revised Quote Book*, p.21
[3] *Creation Ex Nihilo*, vol. 22, no. 1, pp.20–1
[4] Quoted from *The Answers Book*, p.87
[5] Rene Noorbergen, *The Ark File*, London, New English Library, 1980
[6] Fernand Navarra, *The Noah's Ark Expedition*, ed. by Dave Balsiger, London, Coverdale House Publishers, 1974
[7] D Curtis, *Dinosaurs*, Pamphlet no. 275, Portsmouth, Creation Science Movement, p.3

Quotable Quotes

Most people catch their presuppositions from their family and surrounding society the way a child catches measles. But people with more understanding realise that their presuppositions should be chosen after a careful consideration of what world view is true.

> Dr Francis A Schaeffer, *How Should We Then Live?*,
> New Jersey, Fleming H Revell Co., 1976, p.20

While the contradiction between evolutionary thinking and the Bible certainly provides theological grounds for rejecting evolution, many famous scientists have argued strongly against evolution on scientific grounds.

> Ann Lamont, *21 Great Scientists who Believed the Bible*,
> Acacia Ridge, Qld, Answers in Genesis, 1995, p.10

The biblical message is truth and it demands a commitment to truth. It means that everything is not the result of the impersonal plus time, plus chance, but that there is an infinite-personal God who is the Creator of the universe, the space-time continuum. We should not forget that this was what the founders of modern science built upon. It means the acceptance of Christ as saviour and Lord, and it means living under God's revelation.

> Francis A Schaeffer, *How Should We Then Live?*,
> New Jersey, Fleming H Revell Co., 1976, p.252

I have spent so much time in my own writing exploring Job's questions. Many scholars believe it to be the oldest recorded story in the Bible, brilliant drama pre-dating even Abraham. Job strips a relationship with God to its bare essentials: one man alone, naked, having it out with his God. In a pattern that recurs throughout the Old Testament, God stacks the odds against himself in favour of human freedom, and the very fact that the Bible includes Job, with its powerful arguments against God's [seeming]* injustice, underscores that pattern.

> Philip Yancey, *The Bible Jesus Read*, Grand Rapids,
> Zondervan, 1999, p.10 *in brackets my addition

There are some sciences that may be learned by the head, but the science of Christ crucified can only be learned by the heart.

C H Spurgeon (1834–1892), taken from *The Lion Christian Quotation Collection*, Oxford, Lion Publishing, 1997

IX

The Incredible Accuracy of the Bible

Below I select just a few of the many verses from the Bible that show its accuracy in scientific matters.

The Earth is a sphere
Isaiah 40:22:* 'It is He who sits above the circle of the earth.' The Earth being a sphere revolving round the sun was possibly known by our earliest ancestors thousands of years before Copernicus published his thesis *Concerning the Revolutions of the Heavenly Sphere* in 1640.

Countless stars
Genesis 15:5: 'Look towards heaven, and count the stars if you are to number them.' Genesis 22:17: 'I will multiply your descendants as the stars of heaven and as the sand which is on the seashore.' Astronomers calculate there are at least 100 million galaxies like our Milky Way, and possibly as many stars as there are particles of sand on the seashore!

Haematology
Leviticus 17:11, 14: 'For the life of the flesh is in the blood … for it is the life of all flesh. Its blood sustains its life.' William Harvey is credited with the discovery of the circulation of the blood in 1628, over 3,000 years after Moses wrote Leviticus under divine inspiration.

Hydrology
Job 28:24–27: 'God, he looks to the ends of the earth, and sees under the whole heavens, to establish a weight for the wind and mete out waters by measure.' Dr Henry M Morris explains the connection between this verse and hydrology: 'We now know that the global

---

* NB: Unless otherwise stated, all quotations pp.89–90 are from the *Revised Authorised Version* of the Bible.

weights of air and water must be in critical relationship to each other, and to the earth as a whole, to maintain life on earth.'[1]

Geomorphology
Job 14:18–19: 'But as a mountain falls and crumbles away, and as a rock is moved from its place; as water wears away stones and as torrents wash away soil of the earth…'

Astrophysics
Job 9:8–9, 'He [God] alone spreads out the heavens, and treads on the waves of the sea. He made Bear, Orion and the Pleiades.' Read also Job 38:33.

Hygiene
Deuteronomy 23:12–14 gives instructions for disposal of bodily waste. Leviticus 11–14 gives instructions how to recognise and to isolate infectious skin diseases. The same chapters give advice on antenatal care, provision of clean water and how to treat mildew.

Marriage and sexual relations
Leviticus 18–20 gives God's laws on sexual relationships and Exodus 20:14 prohibits sexual intercourse outside marriage. Marriage is defined by Jesus Christ in Matthew 19:3–6 and He refers His hearers back to the foundation of marriage in Genesis 1:27, 2:23–25, 5:1–2.

God made these laws in order that we may be protected from some of the most common diseases and to keep them brings His peace and blessing on our lives.

There are many references in the Bible to health, hygiene, diet, thermodynamics and many other scientific matters which point to its divine authorship.

The following reference in the Bible may become fact in our day

Revelation 13:17 (*New International Version*): 'so that no one could buy or sell unless he had the mark…' may be a reference to the plastic cards we today use for goods and services. Also, giving a direct debit to a financial house precipitates a regular computer-generated transaction. In a 'cashless society' without the use of plastic cards or electronic transfers being accepted, a person could possibly find it difficult to survive unless they were self-sufficient! Already many supermarkets are not taking cheques (next step cash) and many services will not accept cash (BT)!

Ten scientific reasons for a young Earth

If the Earth were millions or billions of years old then:

1. too much salt would have accumulated in the sea, making life impossible

2. the mountains would have been eroded down by weather action

3. for the same reasons rivers would have ceased to flow

4. the Earth by now would be very cold, owing to the cooling of the sun

5. our atmosphere would contain too much helium, making life impossible

6. the world's population would have outgrown our planet

7. the Earth's magnetic field would have been too great for life to exist over ten thousand years ago

8. oil and coal deposits would have dissipated through permeable rocks

9. it takes only a few years for stalactites and stalagmites to form: if the Earth were millions/billions of years old, none of these would be visible, as the process would have ceased many years ago once the caves had been completely filled with lime

10. leaching of gases, etc. from the Earth and its decaying vegetation over millions/billions of years would have polluted the atmosphere, making human life impossible

More about these and others reasons for a young Earth in the booklists and in Looking for Help.

The Bible and mathematics

It is an interesting fact that both the languages in which the original manuscripts of the Bible were written have a numerical value for each letter. As far as I am aware there are no other languages of this type. Each Hebrew letter of the Old Testament has a value and the same is true of the New Testament Greek. There is no space in the text of this book to explain all that can be said about this exciting aspect of the Bible. There are hidden messages in the pages of the Bible, but they do not add any doctrine or information that cannot be easily learnt from the translated text. Ancient Hebrew scholars were intrigued by this discovery. The most notable was Rabbi Moses Ben Maimon, who lived in the twelfth century. One of the best textbooks on this subject is *Cosmic Codes: Hidden Messages from the Edge of Eternity* by Chuck Missler (Koinonia House). These messages have been put there by Almighty God perhaps to encourage our faith in an era of atheism. None of God's servants to whom He dictated His words could have known of these hidden messages and it would have taken any man thousands of years to write a coherent prose containing these messages.

There are other messages which are not mathematical, one being the promise of a redeemer in the meaning of the names of the pre-flood patriarchs. This message would have been an encouragement to Noah, his sons and those who came after them.

The most remarkable mathematical code hidden in the Hebrew and Greek text is the value of π and 'e' in the numerical value of both letters and words of Genesis 1:1 and John 1:1, respectively. The calculations can be found in CSM Pamphlet 337 by Dr Peter Bluer. Only God who is a great mathematician could have implanted these codes in the text for an age when the numerical value of these two constants would be known to man.

The Book of Job

Possibly written after Noah's flood but before Abram (it makes no mention of Mosaic Law), Job gives many indications of an insight into scientific facts thousands of years before they were 'accepted officially'. I recommend anyone studying science reads

Dr Henry M Morris's book *The Remarkable Record of Job*. The back cover states:

> Far from being an engaging fable, the account of Job in the Bible is one of the most historically and scientifically accurate records of the ancient world. Perhaps the oldest book in the Bible, the Book of Job touches on many subjects of science and history: an ice age and hydrologic processes in the oceans, to accounts of cave-dwelling people ... it attests to the historicity of a man named Job who understood at the end of his life that God cannot be 'figured out', but He can most certainly be trusted.

Thousands of years ago, Job and Elihu anticipated God's promise of the resurrection in bodily form and life everlasting (Job 14:14). Job, particularly, was a man of great faith, when all went sour; he lost everything he held dear, he was able to say with firm conviction, 'Though he slay me, yet will I hope in him' (Job 13:15). The prophet Ezekiel (14:14–20) wrote that Job was justified (means: just as if I'd never sinned) by God because of his faith. We can never justify ourselves before God by our works; we are only justified by placing our faith in God's sacrifice of His own Son, the Lord Jesus Christ on the cross, as being the only effective offering for our sin.

The Book of Job shows the suffering that Job endured and his eventual blessing, but does not give us the answers to why God allows suffering. Yet we can be assured that He is with us in all aspects of life.

Job was able to say with great faith, 'Oh that my words were recorded, that they were written on a scroll, that they were inscribed with an iron tool on lead or engraved in rock for ever!' His words were recorded and over the years men and women of faith in the living God can should with great acclamation, 'I know that my Redeemer lives, and that in the end he will stand on the earth. And after my skin has been destroyed, yet in my flesh I will see God. I myself will see him with my own eyes' (Job 19:23–27). How did Job know that he would see the promised one, Jesus Christ (Messiah), and that although his body would return to dust, he would be given a resurrection body? He knew this only by divine revelation.

The Gospel of Jesus Christ gives us great hope; the teaching of evolution in whatever guise can only bring despondency and a sense of hopelessness. Its teaching may be the cause of depression leading to the increased numbers of suicides among the youth in our land. It must grieve the Holy Spirit when we no longer trust every part of God's Word as being the Truth, and this is possibly why the Church in the West no longer experiences the blessing it once did.

Notes

[1] Dr Henry M Morris, *The Remarkable Record of Job*, Green Forest AR, Master Books, 2000, p.37

Weekend Reading
from the Select Bibliography

And God Said… Science Confirms the Authority of the Bible,
Dr Farid Abu-Rahme,
Kilmarnock, John Ritchie Ltd, 1997

Is life a miracle or did it just happen? This is just one of many
questions answered in this book with great clarity. With degrees
in civil engineering, Dr Abu-Rahme is well qualified to give a
scientific assessment of the biblical Noah's Ark and the many
other subjects covered in this book. All through the book, his
personal faith in the living God who speaks through the Bible
shines forth. All 130 pages are packed with helpful information.
And God Said has been translated into over a dozen languages.

Part Three

Quotable Quotes

FIVE PRINCIPLES OF FAITH FROM THE JEWISH PRAYER BOOK

1. I believe with perfect faith that the Creator, blessed be his name, is the Author and Guide of everything that has been created, and that he alone has made, does make, and will make all things.

2. I believe with perfect faith that the Creator, blessed be his name, is a Unity, and that there is no unity in any manner like unto his, and that he alone is our God, who was, is, and will be.

3. I believe with perfect faith that the Creator, blessed be his name, is not a body and that he has not any form whatsoever.

4. I believe with perfect faith that the Creator, blessed be his name, is the first and the last.

5. I believe with perfect faith that to the Creator, blessed be his name, and to him alone it is right to pray, and that it is not right to pray to any besides him.

> Taken from the Thirteen Principles of Faith,
> Daily Prayer Book of the United Hebrew
> Congregations of the British Empire (1935 Edition),
> formulated by Moses Maimonides in the twelfth century

Christianity has fought, still fights and will fight science to the desperate end over evolution, because evolution destroys utterly and finally the very reason Jesus' earthly life was supposedly made necessary. Destroy Adam and Eve and the original sin, and in the rubble you will find the sorry remains of the Son of God. If Jesus was not the redeemer who died for our sins, and this is what evolution means, then Christianity is nothing.

> G Richard Bozarth, 'The Meaning of Evolution',
> *American Atheist*, 20 September 1979, p.30

Not only did JEHOVAH Elohim delight to enrich – even enrapture – with such manifestations of his divine goodness, but he *willed* to do so: it was his *desire* that Adam should enjoy such abundance in the garden of Delight, knowing his love for man.

Even the provision of food – so lowly a matter in such a divine context – expressed the care and solicitude of JEHOVAH Elohim down to the very hairs upon the head of man. He gave Adam to consume no mere bread and water, but *every* tree that was *good* for food.

Nothing was eked out: niggardliness was unknown. Only that man had what was good. No good thing was withheld from the man whom JEHOVAH Elohim had formed, who walked in his innocence.

Then where is this doctrine of devils that parodies man as if evolving from some moron-like ape, scraping a pit of moss for grubs, tearing with bloody hands at some gory carcase? Where is this damnable conjuring of some half-bestial creature, aimlessly wandering in a hideous wilderness, or floundering in some monstrous swamp?

Where? And where the primitive gruntings, the purposeless meanderings, the dread fear of a something, little more than an alien force in the dark, working against man, and against whom man must work to survive his meaningless span? Where? Nowhere but in the lies of Satan ingrained in the depraved mind of man in the darkness of the Fall.

John Metcalfe, *Creation*, Penn,
The Publishing Trust, 1996, pp.105–106

X

Was Adam of the Book of Genesis a Real Man?

Jesus said 'at the beginning of creation God made them male and female' (Mark 10:6). The twenty-four-hour clock started for man when God created Adam. The human race is very much more recent if you believe the Bible, the authoritative Word of God. The trouble we have is our thinking is being conditioned into believing all is millions of years old by the media, which are driven by atheistic evolutionist views.

Jude verse 14 refers to Enoch the seventh from Adam. This is strong New Testament evidence for the fact that genealogies in Genesis 5–11 (repeated in 1 Chronicles 1 and Luke 3; Mary's line, Cainan, is not in earliest manuscripts) contained no breaks. New Testament writers took Genesis literally. Genesis (chapters 5–11) gives the genealogical line from Adam to Abram, a period of 2,200 years. Abraham (as he was renamed by God) historians agree, lived around 2000 BC. Therefore Adam was created about 6,200 years ago (sorry, I don't know the exact year, time of day or date like a certain noble Bishop and would not be as foolish to speculate).

In his book *Genesis for Today*, Dr Andy McIntosh poses these questions which those who profess to love our Lord Jesus Christ and obey His Word should answer:

> Firstly, were it not for the desire of some to disprove Genesis, nobody would normally read Genesis without the obvious impli-cation that here indeed was a tight history. Secondly, I would enquire of all those with a belief in Scripture being the inspired Word of God, would one not expect that the Divinely perfect and accurate scriptural records would correct other ancient writings, and *not the other way round*?[1]

Methuselah lived 969 years, Terah (Abraham's father) only 205 years and in King David's time the lifespan was seventy years. Why the decrease in longevity? This is most possibly due to the change in atmospheric pressure and decreased oxygen in the atmosphere after Noah's flood. Also, when the vapour canopy collapsed there was little protection from harmful radiation. After the flood, lifespan rapidly decreased, suggesting that the side effects of the tragic flood were accumulating. Some have suggested that the extraordinary length of life was due to a different method of calculating age. There is no evidence from the Bible, history or anthropology that this was so.

When Joseph introduced his father, Jacob, to the King of Egypt, the Bible records this very informative conversation. The King asked Jacob. 'How old are you?' Jacob answered, 'My life of wandering has lasted a hundred and thirty years. Those years have been few and difficult, unlike the long years of my ancestors in their wanderings' (Genesis 47:8–9, *Good News Bible*). Jacob lived seventeen years in Egypt and died there aged 147. It is interesting that Jacob considered that his years were few compared to his ancestors and it is obvious he knew of their great age compared to his.

Adam and Eve: no gibbering apes

'Oetzi the Iceman' (estimated to be 5,300 years old) was recently discovered in a glacier on the borders of Italy and Austria. He died at the age of forty-six and was 159 cm tall. He was a highly intelligent craftsman, a good communicator and was extremely organised. Scientists, according to *The Times* (18 December 2000), cannot agree on his diet. James Dickson of Glasgow University has refuted claims made by American scientists that 'Oetzi' was a herbivore. The Bible teaches that from the earliest of times men were highly intelligent. Cain built a large *village with a watchtower* (italics possibly a better translation than 'city' of Genesis 4:17) and Tubal-Cain was a craftsman in bronze and iron (4:22). Tubal-Cain was a son of murderer Lamech, eight generations from Adam.

Because of intense evolutionary indoctrination, many people today think that our generation is the most intelligent that has ever lived on this planet. But just because we have jet airplanes and computers, it does not mean we are the most intelligent. Modern technology results from the accumulation of knowledge. We stand on the shoulders of those who have gone before us. Our brains have suffered from 6,000 years (since Adam) of the Curse. We are greatly degenerated compared with people many generations ago. We may be nowhere near as intelligent or inventive as Adam and Eve's children.

The Answers Book[2]

God created man in His own image and man was perfect. We should not think that Adam and Eve were like apes; before they sinned they were perfect physically and mentally and had a unique relationship with God. That is why the fall is so tragic. Some scholars now think that Genesis 5:1, 'Here is the genealogy of Adam', indicates that the 'genealogy book' in Genesis was actually written by Adam. Before the flood, men lived in a very different world from ours; even after Adam sinned it was almost a perfect world! It took time for God's curse to take effect and, as has already been explained, the great flood changed the topography, climate and geology of the Earth for ever.

Adam and Eve lived in a perfect environment. They needed no artificial heat to keep them warm or electricity to drive gadgets to amuse them. They did not need transport, as they lived in a closely knit community and the ground produced plenty of food for the few inhabitants, so no food technology was needed. Because of Adam's sin and its consequences – the new, hostile environment – man has continually had to drive himself forward to overcome problems which threaten his existence. From this has come the harnessing of energy to keep warm and to cook otherwise unpalatable food; the need to communicate and travel has brought about the discovery of the wheel, the jet engine and telecommunications, to name but a few inventions. The means of storing ideas, inventions and knowledge in written form has possibly had the greatest impact on man developing the lifestyle he has today. Adam and Eve, until they sinned, had no compelling needs that would drive them on to new inventions or discoveries because of their unique relationship with God and the perfect world in which they lived. Don't you envy them?

Adam was a special act of a creative God. All creation, including man, was a deliberate act of God. Read Genesis 1:26. 'All things were made through him [Jesus] and without him nothing was made that was made' (John 1:3, *Revised Authorised Version*). We did not evolve by chance or by a process of natural selection from a so-called 'prebiotic soup of organic molecules', a phrase coined by Dr Leslie Orgel in 1982.

> The more statistically improbable a thing is, the less can we believe that it just happened by blind chance. Superficially the obvious alternative to chance is an intelligent Designer.
>
> Dr Richard Dawkins[3]

Writing about evolution in *Nature*, Sir Fred Hoyle (Professor of Astronomy at Cambridge University) said, 'The chance that higher life forms might have emerged in this way is comparable with the chance that a tornado sweeping through a junkyard might assemble a Boeing 747 from the materials therein.'[4]

According to the Apostle Paul as guided by the Holy Spirit, writing to the Church in Colosse (read chapter 1), God had thoughts about man before He created him. It was man's eternal purpose He had in mind. There was purpose and design in God's creation. God left nothing to chance. The Apostle Paul wrote to Titus that *our faith and hope rests on God who does not lie, who promised eternal life before time began* (see Titus 1:2).

The last of God's creative acts on the sixth day was Adam. Nothing He created was as complex and as wonderful as man; not chance, but deliberate act of creation. The wonder of man – God's creation. God breathed life into him.

> Man is a wonderfully inconceivably complex being. Consider the facts: A chemical factory, an electrical network, climate control, filtration plant – all these controlled centrally by the brain, a thinking computer with the additional ability of loving and hating. Our organism keeps itself alive for several decades and, through various control mechanisms, operates almost without friction. We consist of a hundred million million microscopic

parts, all of which are fantastically fine tuned to, and co-operatively integrated with, each other. When healthy, these parts are continuously rejuvenated and can even repair themselves. This entire marvellous body is kept in operation by a fist-sized pump, the heart, which beats 100,000 times a day and transports nourishment throughout the entire body by means of five litres of blood. The volume of air passing through our lungs during the course of a day is about 20,000 litres. This provides the necessary oxygen, and the unwanted gases are exhaled at the same time. The normal operating temperature is 37 degrees Celsius.

Werner Gitt, *The Wonder of Man*[5]

According to the Bible his body kept on working for Adam a cool 930 years. Our complex bodies show that it was designed by God whose thoughts are not like ours. 'O Lord, how great are your works! Your thoughts are very deep' (Psalm 92:5, *Revised Authorised Version*).

God created Adam in His own image

We are taught through the media, schools and colleges and often in church that we evolved from other life forms like apes or, if you listen to David Attenborough, by natural selection from sea creatures that crawled on to dry land.

Charles Darwin wrote, 'To suppose that the eye with all its inimitable contrivances for adjusting focus to different distances, for admitting different amounts of light, and for the correction of spherical and chromatic aberration, could have been formed by natural selection, seems, I freely confess, absurd in the highest degree.'[6] Charles Darwin had very grave doubts about his theory, which was hijacked by atheists like Thomas Huxley.

God created Adam in His own image (Genesis 1:27) and not in the image of animals which would have been the case if He had intended us to evolve from other species such as apes. Other living creatures (species) were separate creative acts on days five and six (Genesis 1:23–24).

We are people who have a spiritual dimension and we are only complete when we are in a vital, living relationship with God. 'Man is described in the Bible as having been made in "the image of God" (Genesis 1:26, 27). By reason of his creation in this outstanding manner, man is a glorious being possessing spiritual kinship with God.[7]

Once sin entered the world through Adam, the image of God was marred. We had to wait for Jesus Christ, the second Adam, before again any person was in the image of God. Read Hebrews 1:1–3 to learn about the incarnation.

We are so often told that Adam and Eve and the fall are just the elements of a story to illustrate a spiritual point, but the evidence points to it all having happened. If we know anything of the work of the Devil then it was he who tried to scupper God's creation and plan for His people and spread lies about the first eleven chapters of Genesis. But God's plan for man was not thwarted. The Apostle Peter writes in his first letter to the Church that our salvation was put into God's plan before He began his creative work. Writing of Jesus he says, 'He was chosen before the creation of the world, but was revealed in these last times for your sake' (1 Peter 1:20).

What else can the 'image of God' mean? God is spirit; He cannot be seen, although in Jesus He took on the form of a man.

Like God we can communicate – Adam conversed with God (Genesis 2:23). He certainly could talk intelligently. I wonder what Adam said when he first saw Eve! Like God we can think and evaluate – Adam named the animals (Genesis 2:20).

Like God we can write. God wrote with His finger on the wall at Belshazzar's feast and Jesus wrote in the sand when a woman was brought before Him in adultery. Could Adam write? Bible scholars have made a very good case for Adam having written, as dictated by God, the creation account, which we read in Genesis chapter 1 through to chapter 2, verse 7. If it had not been written down soon after creation then it would have been after the style of other ancient accounts of creation. The Genesis account has all the evidence that the author was there when it happened – God! Like God we have our own will – we can see this all too clearly in Adam. Like God we can evaluate and judge. Like God we can love and have the capacity to respond to love. Like God we can be faithful and true. We have the capacity to love and be loved. Like God we are creative beings. Probably this is what distinguishes us particularly from animals, more than any other characteristic. We only need to look about us. Many animals and birds build their homes, but man is much more creative than that. I stand back and look in awe at the many good things man has created which set him far above the ability of animals.

Man promoted to a greater position

People often ask, why did God allow Adam to sin? Surely He could have intervened. God provided salvation from sin in the sacrifice of Jesus on the cross; that was the means, not the end, of His design for man. Recently, because of the progress of stem cell research, there has been talk about the possibility of man living to the ages mentioned in the early chapters of Genesis. In the perfect environment that Adam lived in, he could no doubt have lived longer than he did. In an imperfect world, to live as long as he did would be hell. I cannot think of anything worse than to live in a world as we have today for a thousand years, even if my body worked perfectly. That would not be heaven.

Because of the cross we are reconciled to God, but much comes from that reconciliation, more than we could receive living a thousand years on Earth. The Apostle Paul makes it very clear in his letter to the Christians in Ephesus the great gain that has come to us through this new relationship with God, which even Adam in his perfect state could never experience:

> In the Messiah he chose us in love before the creation of the universe to be holy and without defect in his presence. He determined in advance through Yeshua [Jesus] the Messiah we would be his sons – in keeping with his pleasure and purpose (chapter 1, verses 4 and 5).
>
> Also in union with him we were given an inheritance, we who were picked in advance according to the purpose of the One who effects everything in keeping with the decision of his will, so that we who earlier had put our hope in the Messiah would bring him praise commensurate with his glory (chapter 1, verses 11–12).
>
> God raised us up with the Messiah Yeshua [Jesus] and seated us with him in heaven, in order to exhibit in the ages to come how infinitely rich is his grace, how great is his kindness towards us who are united with Messiah Yeshua (chapter 2, verses 6 and 7).

Quotations from *The Complete Jewish Bible*[8]

It is quite clear that, by God's act of grace, believers have been raised to a new level far more desirous than that occupied by Adam before he sinned. God has made us holy, acceptable to Him, He has made us sons and co-heirs with Jesus. In the new Earth there will be an environment that is indescribable because it will be with Him. This new creation of which we will be part surpasses any creation that has gone before. These things Paul can only describe as 'the incomparable riches of his grace'. If you are a believer you should thank God for His grace. If you are not a believer you should earnestly seek God's gift of grace.

Notes

[1] Dr A McIntosh, *Genesis for Today*, Hereford, Day One Publications, 2006, p.51

[2] *The Answers Book*, p.128

[3] Dr Richard Dawkins, 'The Necessity of Darwinism', *New Scientist*, vol. 94, 15 April 1982, p.130

[4] Sir Fred Hoyle, 'Hoyle on Evolution', *Nature*, vol. 294, 12 November 1981

[5] Gitt, *The Wonder of Man*, p.8

[6] Charles Darwin, *The Origin of Species*, London, J M Dent and Sons Ltd, 1971, p.167

[7] Dr E F Kevan, *Salvation*, London, Evangelical Press, 1973, p.11

[8] David H Stern, *The Complete Jewish Bible*, Clarksville, Jewish New Testament Publications, Inc., 1998

Quotable Quotes

Reason indeed is a goodly gift, and of royal extraction; but, since the fall, it is like Mephibosheth, lame in both its feet.

Rev. Daniel Rowland, 1713–1790,
preaching on Matthew 2:8–9

The fall of man is written in too legible (bold) characters ... those that deny it, by their denying prove it. The very heathens confessed and bewailed it; they could see the streams of corruption running through the whole race of mankind, but could not trace them to the fountainhead. Before God gave a revelation of his Son, man was a riddle to himself. And Moses unfolds more, in one chapter (out of which this text is taken) than all mankind could have been capable of finding out for themselves, though they had studied to all eternity.

In the preceding chapter he had given us a full account how God spake the world into being; and especially how he formed man of the dust of the earth, and breathed into him the breath of life, so that he became a living soul. A council of the Trinity was called concerning the formation of this lovely creature. The result of that council was, 'Let us make man in our image, after our likeness. So God created man in his own image, in the image of God created he him.' Moses remarkably repeats these words, that we might take particular notice of our divine Original. Never was so much expressed in so few words.

Rev. George Whitefield, 1714–1770,
preaching on Genesis 3:15

Therefore, just as sin entered the world through one man, and death through sin, and in this way death came to all men ... For if the many died by the trespass of one man, how much more did God's grace and the gift that came by the grace of the one man, Jesus Christ, overflow to many!

Romans 5:12, 15

...whereby man is very far gone from original righteousness, and is of his own nature inclined to evil, so that the flesh lusteth always contrary to the spirit; and therefore in every person born into this world, it deserveth God's wrath and damnation ... although there is no condemnation for them that believe...

39 Articles of Religion 1662, (part article 9), the Church of England

Seek a good wife of thy God, for she is the best gift of his providence; Yet ask not in bold confidence that which he hath not promised: Thou knowest not his good will: be thy prayer then submissive thereunto; And leave thy petition to his mercy, assured that He will deal well with thee if thou are to have a wife of thy youth, she is now living on earth; Therefore think of her, and pray for her weal [health]; yea, though thou hast not seen her.

Martin F Tupper, *Of Marriage, Proverbial Philosophy*, London, T Hatchard, 1854. This poem was shown to Susannah by the Baptist preacher C H Spurgeon on his proposal of marriage at Crystal Palace, 10 June 1854

XI

Adam the Unique Man

Five aspects of His uniqueness

We are all unique, in that we are different from one another –
even identical twins. But Adam was unique in five ways (there
may be others) from all who were to follow him. If mankind
evolved from other species, Adam must have descended, therefore been born, which is contrary to Bible teaching.

1. ADAM WAS CREATED – NOT BORN OF A WOMAN
   (READ GENESIS 1:27)

In Genesis 1:27 we read that God created man. Then in Genesis
2:18 we can see that God created Adam first. Everyone since
Adam and Eve has been born of a woman. We hear so much from
the media that mankind has evolved. Today folk are really
confused about God's creation, because they have been taught
atheistic evolution in school or college, and daily through the
media, and then they read the Genesis account. Often we
compound their confusion by saying that the theory of evolution
is somehow compatible with the Genesis record. Some go down
the road of teaching theistic evolution, and somehow sandwich in
a time span of billions of years, with dinosaurs before Adam early
on in chapter 1 of Genesis before day six when man was created.
This is just not honest, because the ancient text does not allow us
to do that, and distinctly makes clear that before Adam sinned
there was no death. Adam's sin introduced death, destruction and
trouble. We are living on a fossil graveyard that post-dates Adam
and was the result of his sin.

If people ask me how I reconcile Genesis with evolution, I tell
them, I don't! I believe the theory of evolution is in error; it is a
lie from the Devil himself. I tell them that what is in the first

eleven chapters of Genesis actually took place and I refer them to the genealogy of Adam in chapter 5. Then I give answers to their questions about science and the meaning of life from what we are taught in the Bible. I have never been laughed at by enquirers, but only by Christians who have never bothered to read books other than those that go down the broad 'Evolution Way'. I challenge all who think the world and dinosaurs are millions of years old to read some of the books given in the select bibliography at the end of this book.

2.   ADAM WAS NOT AWARE OF ANY NEEDS (READ GENESIS 2:18)

After all had been created Adam had only one outstanding need that God identified – that was a human companion. Adam was unique in that he was alone. Even Noah had his family in the Ark. Adam had no one, he was alone. Adam had no awareness of his need; it is the supreme example of God's character knowing our need before we realise it ourselves.

3.   GOD USED ADAM'S BODY TO CREATE EVE

None of us can claim to have acquired a wife in the way Adam did. In Genesis 2:21–24 we are told exactly how God created this companion for Adam. In verse 24 we are told by God that it is because of this particular act in creating Eve directly from Adam's body while in a deep sleep that there is a special relationship between one man and one woman in matrimony. It is interesting that God took Adam's rib to make Eve. The rib happens to be the most easily regenerated bone in the human body, provided the periosteum is left intact. The periosteum covering the bone manufactures the new cells for new bone growth. The Bible is correct whenever it touches on any scientific matter, but that is not surprising, as it was written by God, who tells no lies. Dr Carl Wieland had bone from his rib taken to help rebuild his face after a major injury in a road accident. Carl Wieland is the founding editor of *Creation Magazine* (Creation International Ministries).

A special spiritual relationship will always be the basis upon which a man and woman come together as one in lifelong union. Jesus quoted this verse, underlining the foundation for marriage.

The foundation of marriage goes back to creation and so does the observance of the need for man to rest one day in seven. God took six days to create and on the seventh He rested, 'stood back', and enjoyed all He had created. God did not completely stop work, He ceased from His creative work. He sustains His creation. Jesus is recorded as saying in John 5:17, 'My Father is always at his work to this very day.' In Genesis 2:3 we read that God blessed the seventh day and set it apart from all the rest of His creative week. Observance of a day of rest was enshrined by God in the Mosaic Law. Since Christ rose from the grave in victory over sin, His followers have kept this day of rest for worship. God's next creative work will be 'the new heaven and the new Earth'.

This cycle of twenty-four hours, six days, plus one of rest, is programmed into man by his creator – I have no doubt it was for Adam, so it must be for us. We ignore it at our cost. Employers and employees take note. Scientists believe that they may have identified a set of clock genes in humans, animals and plants.

4. ADAM WAS NOT BORN – NOR DID HE INHERIT ORIGINAL SIN

From Genesis 1:27–31 we note that everything God created was good – perfect. So here is Adam, a perfect man, a man not marred by sin. There was no barrier of sin between him and God, a unique relationship.

Atheistic evolutionists teach that man is innately good and his environment and nurture are the cause of any failure, but that is in stark contrast to the teaching of the Bible about the nature of man. The Psalmist spoke of us when he wrote, 'Surely I was sinful at birth, sinful from the time my mother conceived me' (Psalm 51:5). Job states: 'Man born of woman is of few days and full of trouble … Who can bring what is pure from the impure?' (Job 14:1, 4). The Apostle Paul wrote, 'We were by nature objects of wrath' (Ephesians 2:3), 'For just as through the disobedience of one man the many were made sinners, so also through the obedience of one man [Jesus Christ] the many will be made righteous' (Romans 5:19). The Bible clearly teaches Adam's sin had an effect on the nature of his descendants, though this is indeed difficult for us to comprehend. Furthermore, Jesus taught that it was necessary for us to go through a spiritual rebirth in order that we may be delivered from God's condemnation (read John 3:1–18).

Adam did not inherit a fallen nature; this is what makes his sin so tragic. Adam could not give 'his inherited nature' as his defence, even though this itself is no defence before a holy God. Adam, when he sinned, must have felt a bitter bereavement. Adam lost his fellowship with God; he was bereaved of that intimate fellowship with his maker; that relationship was never the same again. He had been deceived and, as with all deception, there is loss.

5.   ADAM WAS IN PERFECT FELLOWSHIP WITH GOD

In Genesis 3:8 we learn that Adam and his wife heard God walking in the garden. For Adam to meet God in this way may have been part of life in the garden. It was not that God, their friend, was walking in the garden that terrified Adam and Eve, but that for the first time in their lives they were not ready to meet their creator.

Until Adam sinned he was in perfect fellowship with God. I remember as a child not so much being terrified over what I had done, but being terrified over the knowledge that my mother and father would eventually find out I was the guilty one. A barrier of guilt and shame had for the first time descended on both Adam and Eve, in that idyllic garden where all had been perfect. We cannot begin to understand the depths of how both Adam and Eve must have felt: a crushing sense of loss of fellowship with God. As people inheriting a sinful nature I don't think we really can empathise with Adam. We have never been in a sinless state. What happened in the garden was the most awful tragedy imaginable. All Earthly creation was tainted for ever by the consequence of Adam's sin and the first death of an animal resulted: 'God made garments of skin for Adam and his wife and clothed them' (Genesis 3:21). It was God who made the first sacrifice of an animal.

God is preparing a place for us where we will be in fellowship with Him in a way that we cannot imagine. We shall be in heavenly places with our Lord Jesus Christ, to whom be glory and honour.

Quotable Quotes

God's moral law went all the way back to the Garden of Eden, where (in addition to various other commands concerning sexuality, rest and work), God told Adam and Eve not to eat from the tree of the knowledge of good and evil. Theologians argue about whether or not our first parents also knew any of the Ten Commandments. The Bible simply doesn't say. But whether or not God revealed any of its specific commands, Adam and Eve were ruled by its basic principles; love for God and love for one another. They were obligated to honour one another, to preserve life, and to tell the truth – the kind of conduct later mandated on Mount Sinai. And in their first sin, Adam and Eve managed to violate nearly all ten of God's basic rules. Taking the forbidden fruit was a theft, stimulated by covetous desire, based on a lie about God's character. Eating it was a way of having another god. It was also tantamount to murder because it led to the death of the entire human race. From the beginning our first parents were bound by the basic principles of what theologians call 'the law of creation' or the 'law of nature'.

> Philip Graham Ryken, *Written in Stone: The Ten Commandments and Today's Moral Crisis*, Wheaton, Crossway Books, 2003, Chapter 1, p.19

The condition of Man after the fall of Adam is such that he cannot turn and prepare himself, by his own natural strength and good works, to faith and calling upon God: Wherefore we have no power to do good works pleasant and acceptable to God, without the grace of God by Christ preventing [going before us and helping] us, that we may have a good will, and working with us, when we have that good will.

> Articles of Religion (number 10), *Book of Common Prayer*, 1662, the Church of England

He taught the Scripture doctrine of original sin, which consists in these two things: First, Adam's personal offence imputed; and second, the entire depravity of his fallen nature, imparted to all his seed. By the former we are held faulty and stand guilty in our persons before God; and by the latter our natures are corrupted, prone to sin, and naturally inclined to all evil; and thus it is written: 'By the offence of one, judgement came upon all men to condemnation.' Hence we are all by nature sinners and children of wrath. The Church of England also bears her testimony to the truth of this alarming and awful doctrine in the ninth article of her faith, in which she asserts that 'original sin is the fault and corruption of the nature of every man that naturally is engendered of the offspring of Adam, whereby man is of his own nature inclined to evil,' etc. The fault is from Adam's offence imputed; our corruption, and propensity to evil, is from the depravity of his sinful nature communicated and imparted to us.

Rev. George Whitefield's teaching on the consequences of Adam's fall. Extract from funeral sermon given at Whitefield's funeral by R Elliot

XII

Grave Consequences of the Fall of Adam

It is not difficult to find examples in our world of the widespread effects of the fall. Here are just a few: breakdown of marriage, cruelty to children, corruption in business, bad taste expressed in our culture (like *Big Brother*, *The Jerry Springer Show*, which heap misery upon misery), then our inability to administer the wealth God has given us, so that we have malnutrition and illness over much of the globe. Governments and financial authorities are unable to control greed and dishonesty, bringing about the near collapse of the world's financial system. This greed has made the poor even poorer and will have a long-lasting impact on Third World countries.

The nations of the world are unable to get a consensus on action to halt genocide. In 1994 a UN Peacekeeping Mission was despatched to Rwanda under the command of General Romeo Dallaire. They found themselves powerless in the face of overwhelming violence. General Dallaire said on the BBC Radio 4 *Today* programme (17 May 2007), 'The media were there. No one was listening to the warnings … there was no fundamental will to do anything.' A representative of one country said to the General, 'They are only humans, and there are too many anyway!' If a country has nothing to offer, such as oil or a strategic position, no one goes to their aid. For years the government of Sudan has being practising genocide, hundreds of thousands killed and several millions driven over the border into neighbouring Chad. These people have been barely kept alive by non-governmental organisations, mainly Christian. The United Nations, who act on the consensus of the nations, have failed to take action to stop this killing. The governments of the world are silent! The conflict in this part of Africa continues today.

The effects of the fall are so great that we can no longer see the image of God in the people He created. We could go on and on about the effects of Adam's sin. If we read the first eleven chapters of Genesis we soon become aware that it was Adam's sin that eventually caused the shortening of man's lifespan to three score years and ten. The only hope for the world is the return of our Lord Jesus Christ, who will bring an end to suffering.

I see no reason to doubt the authenticity of the account of Genesis 3 in which Adam and Eve are deceived by a snake. God can speak through Balaam's ass (Numbers 22:28 and 2 Peter 2:16), and Jesus can deliver people from evil spirits and on one occasion send them into a herd of pigs; therefore I believe the account. The Bible teaches that the Devil can take possession of a person who has completely given themselves over to his control (Mark 1:23–27 and Luke 4:33–36), so why not a snake or serpent?

One of the consequences of Adam's sin was God's curse on the Devil and the Earth.

It is well worth taking the time to look at the narrative of Genesis chapter 3, which describes the event of Adam and Eve falling prey to the deception of the serpent. God does not curse them for their action. God's love for His created Adam and his wife Eve never wanes. He curses the Earth and the serpent. God curses the serpent and in doing so curses the Devil. Adam and Eve are given in verse 15 the prophetic promise that the Devil will be inflicted with a mortal blow. This promise was fulfilled several thousand years later when Jesus of Nazareth died on the cross and rose alive in triumph over sin and death from the grave. This is the heart of the Gospel. The end of the Devil is recorded in Revelation 20:1–10.

What was the first sin committed? The sin of doubting God's Word. What did God say to Adam and Eve? 'You shall not eat it, lest you die.' It was their disregard for God's Word that led to their disobedience. It is doubting God's Word, the Bible, that has been the springboard for atheistic teaching on evolution.

I read this in *The Word for Today*: 'The Word of God is the language of the Holy Spirit. When you stay in the Word, you're allowing the Holy Spirit to speak constantly to you.'[1] It is always the disregarding or doubting God's Word that is the sin which brings us into further disobedience. It is when we obey God's

Word that we have fellowship with Him. Adam's sin was questioning what God had said and deciding someone else knew best – the result, disobedience.

It is because we have taken on board the lie of evolution, which is contrary to God's Word, that He is not blessing the Church as in previous times. I believe that like any other sin we must confess it before God and seek His forgiveness.

To summarise: the Scriptures do not accommodate the Theory of Evolution by natural selection. The Hebrew text does not make a gap between the first and second verses of Genesis 1, so we may not insert millions of years. The two accounts of creation in Genesis 1 and 2 are one and the same creation – not separate creative acts. Two separate acts would mean there was death before Adam our ancestor was created, and that is contrary to the teaching of both Old and New Testaments. I have argued against evolutionary teaching not from science but from Scripture. The Bible is the 'God-breathed' inspired Word of God, not inspired like other books from the human imagination, but by the Holy Spirit. The only factual book on creation could only be written by the person who was there and did it all – God! God calls us to believe the truth contained in the Bible. If there is conflict between the Bible and the theories of men, then Christians have no alternative but to accept what the Bible teaches. Remember, the theories of men change from day to day. Anyone who has followed the creation-evolution debate closely will be aware of the shifting position of evolutionary arguments as scientific research brings new facts into consideration.

The story has been told that in successive years Albert Einstein set the same questions for a science examination paper. One bright student pointed this out to Einstein. His reply was that the student was correct, but then Einstein added that the answers would be different. Even Einstein knew that, owing to new scientific discoveries, many of the same questions would have new answers. As time goes by new assessments always have to be made in the light of scientific discoveries.

We have been deluded into believing the 'theory of evolution' as fact through 150 years of unremitting bombardment of atheistic propaganda. This is the main stumbling block to many accepting the Gospel today; and it also throws doubts about the Bible into the minds of people who are seeking the truth about creation and the world in which we live. The Church should not be ashamed of creationist views and should teach that macro-evolution is contrary to Scripture. We have modern scientific evidence that confirms the biblical account of creation and the universal flood, information which many theologians, Warfield, Hodge and others who reluctantly accepted evolution, did not have in their day. Today we are totally without excuse.

All that has gone wrong in our society in recent years points to an abandonment of belief in the reliability of the first eleven chapters of Genesis as a factual account. It is not surprising that marriage, and a day of rest and worship, both of which have their foundations in the first two chapters of Genesis, have largely been abandoned. The Church has lost its power to stop the advance of the influence of forces which may eventually destroy a nation that God has seen fit to bless mightily over four centuries.

The great majority of our population have been brainwashed into thinking that the world is millions of years old, and that there is no God; or that, if it should happen that there is a God who created it, then He is remote and certainly is not interested in us! No wonder so many of our youth are committing suicide because they perceive the hopelessness of life. The truth is: Genesis 1–11 is factual. It dates the special creation of the world as being only thousands of years old, and in it we read of a God who is very much involved in the affairs of men, a God who wants us to have a personal living relationship with Him by faith. He knows we live in a difficult world, but He is on hand to help us. He came to seek and to save those who are lost. He planned our position as co-heirs with His Son before He began His creative work.

The teaching of evolution, including so called 'theistic evolution', is an insult to the Lord Jesus Christ, 'by him all things were created, for him all things were created and by him all things are sustained' (Colossians 1:16–17, author's paraphrase).

Genesis 1–11 does not tell us *why* God created, but the order in which He did it, and it stands up to scientific scrutiny as does the rest of the Word of God. To find out why God created we should read Ephesians 1:4–10 and Colossians 1:12–22. God had a plan and purpose for fallen man long before AD 33, in fact before creation. The objective of God's plan is to raise us up to that of sons (co-heirs), a greater state than Adam and Eve had, even before they sinned. We will return to that in a further chapter.

Notes

[1] *The Word for Today*, United Christian Broadcasters, Stoke-on-Trent, www.ucb.co.uk

XIII

Conclusion: in Jesus a Glorious Future

The Bible is quite clear when it tells us about creation. God was the creator and He did this by His very word of command (2 Peter 3:5–7, Psalm 33:6–9). The Apostle Paul teaches that creation was God's deliberate act (Romans 9:19–22). Creation was His wisdom in action, the writers of the Psalms & Proverbs tell us (Psalm 104:24). The Bible is its own commentator and it contains many references to why God created, how He created and when He created.

It was His design and purpose for greater things to come. It was for the glory of His son our Lord Jesus Christ (Proverbs 8:22–31, Colossians 1:16) and for His people whom He has made heirs with Him and citizens of heaven (Ephesians 2:19). This is an elevation of mankind far above that of the once-sinless Adam. The text from Proverbs quoted refers to God's wisdom.

The central theme running strongly through the Bible is God's revelation of His Son in the redeeming of His chosen people, who are those that have placed their faith in the Lord Jesus Christ.

The Apostle Peter speaks of the 'precious blood of Christ, a lamb without blemish or defect who was chosen before the creation of the world' (1 Peter 1:19–20). There was conscious planning by God; He was not taken by surprise by the events recorded in the earlier chapters of Genesis. Teaching the unproven theory that all that there is came from a single cell by accident rules out God's plan so forcefully put in the Bible. How can anyone still believe in an evolutionary view of how our world came into being? Swapping Bible truth for a theistic evolutionary view is like exchanging an excellent meal in a top restaurant for the slops from its kitchen.

Revelation 13:8 speaks of 'the lamb slain from the creation of the world'. There may be many good scientific reasons why evolution could not take place; I have not argued from that standpoint but have appealed to Scripture, the Bible, which is God's Word to us. God's design is not only evident from DNA, etc., but is revealed to us in the Bible. The design for our lives and our future as Christians is secure in Him, the lamb slain.

Without the act of creation, and the subsequent fall of man, there could be no Good Friday. Dr Martyn Lloyd-Jones in his book *The Cross* states:

> The cross is the most wonderful thing that has ever happened, and it is very important that we should be clear about this ... It is Good Friday because it was the Friday on which the Son of God did that without which none of us could ever be saved. Without that, none of us could ever come to a knowledge of God ... the best day that has ever happened in the history of the human race.[1]

Professor Richard Dawkins in a recent interview on BBC Radio 4 stated that Jesus was the imaginary person of Christians. Many Christians have had such a profound experience of God's grace and mercy in Jesus based on evidence not seen, so that they can say with the Apostle Paul, 'I know whom I have believed, and am convinced that he [Jesus] is able to guard what I have entrusted to him for that day' (2 Timothy 1:12). We can trust this creator God who sent His son into the world to secure our future.

During the Second World War the most awful atrocities were committed, but none worse than those against Jews. Millions were killed. When reading Johanna-Ruth Dobschiner's most moving book *Selected to Live*, about life in Europe for persecuted Jews, I was aware that many of them became atheists and lost any faith they had in God.[2] Yet there was Johanna-Ruth, hidden in a safe house by Christians, who coming across a Bible and by reading alone was brought to a living faith in our Lord Jesus Christ. She lost her family to the gas chambers and many who hid her were shot by the firing squad. It is an amazing record of her finding the Messiah. I urge you to read it. The Bible is the life-giving Word of God, changing lives when the odds are stacked against any hope.

I mention this book because the answer to our problems and

questions are in the Bible alone. We may think we have all the answers to the theory of evolution and atheist answers to our origins in scientific argument, but in the end we must return to the Bible, relying on it as the authoritative Word of the living God, who created everything out of nothing. He had our future in mind when He planned to raise those who trust in His son to glory, as heirs of God.

We have, through the Lord Jesus Christ, been raised to a new position with God greater than that of Adam before he sinned. This new life we shall share with our saviour for eternity, never to be parted again. We shall be living in a new dimension that only God inhabits at present, without the constraints of time and our Earthly bodies. John Newton, the converted slave trader, put it all into words of a hymn:

> 'Tis grace hath brought me safe thus far
> And grace will lead me home...
> When we've been there ten thousand years
> Bright shining as the sun,
> We've no less days to sing God's praise
> Than when we've first begun.

The last words of this chapter must come from our creator God who planned everything for the good of our redemption. But first, what does redemption mean? If you work in the mortgage business you will know what redemption means, or if you bought a house on a mortgage, or, in the days of hire purchase, loans for a car or some valuable article, you may also know. It means 'to buy back'. I remember the day when I redeemed the mortgage. The house that once could have been taken away from me by default was really mine. I was so looking forward to that day that I marked the days off on my calendar and I was overjoyed to receive the letter from the mortgage company asking me where I wanted the deeds deposited. At last, the house was mine. How much greater the anticipation and joy it must be for God, who paid the price with the death of His dear son, the Lord Jesus Christ, when one sinner repents and places their faith in what was done on the cross for them. There is no redemption like the kind that God makes on our behalf:

For in bringing many sons to glory, it was only fitting that God, the Creator and Preserver of everything, should bring the Initiator of their deliverance to the goal through sufferings. For both Yeshua [Jesus], who sets people apart for God, and the ones being set apart have a common origin – this is why he is not ashamed to call them **brothers** [and sisters].

The Complete Jewish Bible, Hebrews 2:10–11

Notes

[1] Dr Martyn Lloyd-Jones, *The Cross*, London, Crossway Books, 1986, p.107
[2] Johanna-Ruth Dobschiner, *Selected to Live*, London, Hodder & Stoughton, 2006

Weekend Reading
from the Select Bibliography

Has Darwin Had His Day?, *What the Scientific Journals Say*
Dr D Rosevear,
Portsmouth, Creation Science Movement, 2007

Dr Bill Cooper, in his recommendation, calls the book a 'gold-mine', which I found it to be. The author draws information from well-known scientific journals to show that Darwin's hypothesis has failed every scientific test to which it has been subjected. It will surprise the reader that the journals often support creationist views. The reader will notice that Dr Rosevear has a lively sense of humour. The 116 pages are interwoven with beautiful colour pictures.

Looking for Help!

Exceptionally Helpful Addresses and Information

Answers in Genesis (AiG)
WEBSITE: www.AnswersInGenesis.com
MAGAZINE: *Answers*, a family magazine, annual subscription for
            four copies
INFO: Provides speakers for meetings

Biblical Foundations
ADDRESS: Dr A J Monty White, PO Box 111, Pontyclun CF72
            0BH
WEBSITE: www.biblicalfoundations.org.uk

Creation Ministries International
WEBSITE: www.creation.com
MAGAZINE: *Creation*, published four times a year. Large, glossy,
            full of excellent articles on creation, science and a
            whole range of matters Christians should know about
INFO: Book/DVD catalogue available; provides speakers
            for meetings

Creation Resources Trust
ADDRESS: PO Box 3237, Yeovil BA22 7WD
WEBSITE: www.c-r-t.co.uk
MAGAZINE: Two specialised publications: *Our World* for
            children and *Original View* for teenagers
INFO: UK Registered Charity; member of the Evangelical
            Alliance; provides detailed list of speakers and seminars;
            no membership subscription, but gifts welcomed

Creation Science Movement
ADDRESS: PO Box 888, Portsmouth PO6 2YD

WEBSITE: www.CreationScienceMovement.com
INFO: A member of the Evangelical Alliance; UK Registered Charity; annual membership – quarterly newsletter and pamphlet; mail order books and catalogue; provides speakers for meetings
AIMS: To show that the Scriptures, and in particular those that bear upon creation, are reliable; to lecture on Creation Science at universities, schools and churches; to publish and distribute the journal, *Creation*, pamphlets, books and video and audio tapes demonstrating that the biblical account of Creation is supported by *true* science. Publishes hundreds of pamphlets to combat the false teaching of the theory of evolution.

Day One Publications
ADDRESS: Ryelands Road, Leominster, Hereford HR6 8NZ
WEBSITE www.dayone.co.uk
INFO: Publishers of many excellent books by scientists Dr Stuart Burgess, Dr Andy McIntosh and others; catalogue and gift ideas available

Genesis EXPO
ADDRESS: 17/18 The Hard, Portsmouth, near Harbour Railway Station, HMS *Warrior* and Portsmouth Dockyard
OPEN: Tuesday–Saturday 10 a.m. to 3 p.m. during the winter, extended times in the summer
INFO: Founded and administered by Creation Science Movement. An exhibition that sets out to demonstrate that the universe and everything in it was designed and created by God. Huge selection of books, booklets, artefacts and gifts. This exhibition is free

Institute for Creation Research (CR)
ADDRESS: PO Box 6607, ElCajon, CA 92021, USA
WEBSITE: www.icr.org
MAGAZINE: Subscription to *Acts and Facts* free

Koinonia House
EBSITE: www.khouse.org
MAGAZINE: *Personal Update* – monthly journal by subscription,
           editors Chuck & Nancy Missler. Gives biblical
           teaching on current affairs, etc.
INFO: Lists of videos, tapes and MP3s; organiser of
           conferences

NPN Videos
ADDRESS: PO Box 2224, Swindon SN6 7LG
WEBSITE: www.christianvideos.co.uk
INFO: Producers of the DVDs *Life's Story* and *Life's Story 2*.
           These are two beautifully filmed wildlife produc-
           tions explaining the origins and purpose of all life

The Banner of Truth Trust
ADDRESS: The Grey House, 3 Murrayfield Road, Edinburgh
           EH12 6EL
WEBSITE: www.banneroftruth.co.uk
INFO: Publishers of Christian literature, including the
           books written by Professor E J Young quoted from
           in this publication

The Evangelical Library
ADDRESS: 5–6 Gateway Mews, Ringway, Bounds Green,
           London N11 2UT
WEBSITE: www.evangelical-library.org.uk
MAGAZINE: *In Writing*
INFO: Over 80,000 books available to borrow on whole
           range of subjects, most by Christian authors;
           sections on Genesis, evolution, creation and
           archaeology, etc.; books can be borrowed by
           visiting or by post; annual membership –
           reduction for students; well worth becoming a
           member

Truth in Science
WEBSITE: www.info@truthinscience.org.uk
INFO: An organisation seeking to promote truthfulness in
           science education

Understand the Times

ADDRESS: PO Box 27239, Santa Ana, CA 92799, USA
WEBSITE: www.understandthetimes.org
INFO: Roger Oakland, biologist and author-lecturer who
            lives in Costa Mesa, California, speaks on the sub-
            ject of how the Bible helps us to understand the
            past, what is happening in the world today, and
            where we are heading in the future. Often speaks in
            the UK. Books, videos and tapes

Books of the Bible

Often referred to as The Scriptures, The Word of God, or God's Word.

The Old Testament books

Genesis	2 Chronicles	Daniel
Exodus	Ezra	Hosea
Leviticus	Nehemiah	Joel
Numbers	Esther	Amos
Deuteronomy	Job	Obadiah
Joshua	Psalms	Jonah
Judges	Proverbs	Micah
Ruth	Ecclesiastes	Nahum
I Samuel	Song of Solomon	Habakkuk
2 Samuel	Isaiah	Zephaniah
I Kings	Jeremiah	Haggai
2 Kings	Lamentation	Zechariah
I Chronicles	Ezekiel	Malachi

The New Testament books

Matthew	Ephesians	Hebrews
Mark	Philippians	James
Luke	Colossians	I Peter
John	I Thessalonians	2 Peter
Acts of the Apostles	2 Thessalonians	I John
Romans	I Timothy	2 John
I Corinthians	2 Timothy	3 John
2 Corinthians	Titus	Jude
Galatians	Philemon	Revelation

Select Bibliography

Charles Darwin

Clark, Ronald W, *The Survival of Charles Darwin*, London, Weidenfeld & Nicolson, 1985

Desmond, Adrian and James Moore, *Darwin*, London, Penguin, 1992

Keynes, Randal, *Annie's Box*, London, Fourth Estate, 2001

McNaughton, Ian and Paul Taylor, *Darwin and Darwinism 150 Years Later*, Hereford, Day One Publications, 2009

Rosevear, Dr D, *Darwin's Change of Heart*, Pamphlet 309, Portsmouth, Creation Science Movement, 1996

Harding, D (ed.), *Interview with C H Spurgeon*, Hereford, Day One Publications, 2006

The Church in the nineteenth century

Carson, John T, *God's River in Spate*, Belfast, Publications Board, Presbyterian Church in Ireland, 1958

Edwards, Brian H, *Revival! A People Saturated with God*, Durham, Evangelical Press, 1990

Orr, Dr Edwin J, *Light of the Nation*, Exeter, Paternoster Press, 1965

Paisley, Dr Ian R K, *The 'Fifty Nine' Revival*, Belfast, Martyrs Memorial Free Presbyterian Church, 1981

Prime, Samuel I, *The Power of Prayer, The New York Revival of 1858*, Edinburgh, The Banner of Truth Trust, 1991

Schaeffer, Dr Francis A, *How Should We Then Live?*, New Jersey, Fleming H Revell Co., 1976

The Bible, Noah's flood and archaeology

Abou-Rahme, Dr Farid, *And God Said: Science Confirms the Authority of the Bible*, Kilmarnock, John Ritchie Ltd, 1997

Ashton, J and David Down, *Unwrapping the Pharaohs*, Arkansas, USA, Master Books, 2008

Bruce, F F, *The Canon Scripture*, Glasgow, Chapter House, 1988

Cooper, Dr Bill, *After the Flood*, Chichester, New Wine Press, 1995

——, *The Early Writing of Genesis*, Pamphlet 377, Portsmouth, Creation Science Movement, 2010

Currid, John D, *Study Commentary on Genesis*, Darlington, Evangelical Press, 2003

Edwards, Brian H and Clive Anderson, *Through the British Museum with the Bible*, Hereford, Day One Publications, 2008

Daniell, David, *The Bible in English*, New Haven and London, Yale University Press, 2003

Gurney, R, *Six-day Creation: Does it Matter what you Believe?*, Hereford, Day One Publications, 2007

Lloyd-Jones, D M, *The Gospel in Genesis*, Hereford, Day One Publications, 2010

McIntosh, Dr A, *Genesis for Today*, Hereford, Day One Publications, 2006

Morris, Dr Henry M, *The Genesis Record*, Grand Rapids MI, USA, Baker Book House Co., 1998

——, *The Remarkable Record of Job*, Green Forest AR, USA, Master Books, 2000

——, *Biblical Creationism, what each book of the Bible teaches about creation and the flood*, Green Forest AR, USA, Master Books, 2000

Patten, Eugene P, Richard V Hatch and Kenneth W Steinhauer, *The Long Day of Joshua & Six Other Catastrophes*, Seattle, Pacific Meridian Publishing Co., 1977

Peet, J H John, *In the Beginning God Created*, London, Grace Publications, 1994

Ryken, Philip Graham, *Written in Stone*, Wheaton, Crossway Books, 2003

Velikovsky, I, *Worlds in Collision*, New York, Doubleday, 1949

——, *Ages in Chaos*, London, Sidgwick & Jackson, 1953

Weber, K, *The Lord of the Sabbath*, Hereford, Day One Publications, 2007

Whitcomb, John C, *The World that Perished*, Grand Rapids MI, Baker Book House, 1973

Whitcomb, John C and Henry M Morris, *The Genesis Flood*, New Jersey, The Presbyterian & Reformed Publishing Co., 1961

Winsbury, Leigh, 'Noah's Ark Found?', *Creation* (Portsmouth, Creation Science Movement), vol. 16, no. 8, May 2010

Wiseman, P J, *Clues to Creation in Genesis*, London, Marshall Paperbacks, 1977

——, *Creation Revealed in Six Days*, London, Marshall Morgan & Scott, 1949

Wiseman, D J, *Illustrations from Biblical Archaeology*, London, The Tyndale Press, 1958

Yancey, Philip, *The Bible Jesus Read*, Grand Rapids, Zondervan, 1999

Young, Dr E J, *In the Beginning*, Edinburgh, The Banner of Truth Trust, 1976

——, *Thy Word is Truth*, Edinburgh, The Banner of Truth Trust, 1997

——, *The Way Everlasting*, Edinburgh, The Banner of Truth Trust, 1997

The Bible and mathematics

Anderson, David, *Creation and Mathematics*, Pamphlet 370, Portsmouth, Creation Science Movement, 2008

Bluer, Dr Peter, *Pi and the Earth's Orbit*, Pamphlet 319, Portsmouth, Creation Science Movement, 1998

——, *The Two Universal Constants Encoded in Genesis 1:1 & John 1:1*, Pamphlet 337, Portsmouth, Creation Science Movement, 2001

Gray, Matthew M A, *The Value of Pi & the Bible*, Pamphlet 330, Portsmouth, Creation Science Movement, 2000

Missler, Chuck, *Hidden Treasures in the Biblical Text*, Coeur d'Alene ID, Koinonia House, 2004

——, *Cosmic Codes, Hidden Messages from the Edge of Eternity*, Coeur d'Alene ID, Koinonia House, 2001

The Big Bang and astronomy

Burgess, Dr S, *He Made the Stars Also*, Hereford, Day One Publications, 2001

DeYoung, Dr Ronald B, *Astronomy and the Bible*, Grand Rapids MI, Baker Book House Co, 2000

Humphries, Dr Russell, *Starlight and Time*, Green Forest AR, Master Books, 1994

Morris, John, *Is the Big Bang Biblical?*, Green Forest AR, USA, Master Books, 2004

Williams, A and Dr J Hartnett, *Dismantling the Big Bang*, Green Forest AR, Master Books, 2006

Design in creation

Burgess, Dr S, *Hallmarks of Design*, Hereford, Day One Publications, 2004

Snow, P, *The Design and Origin of Birds*, Hereford, Day One Publications, 2006

Gitt, Dr Werner, *The Wonder of Man*, Bielefeld, Christliche Literature-Verbreitung, 2003

The creation vs. evolution debate

Bigalke, R, *The Genesis Factor: Myths and Realities*, Arkansas, Master Books, 2008

Blick, Dr Edward F, *A Scientific Analysis of Genesis*, Oklahoma, Hearthstone Publishing, 1991

Bowden, M, *Ape–Men: Fact or Fallacy*, Bromley, Sovereign Books, 1997

———, *Science vs. Evolution Fraud*, Bromley, Sovereign Books, 1991

———, *True Science Agrees with the Bible*, Bromley, Sovereign Books, 1998

Burgess, Dr S, *The Origin of Man – The Image of an Ape or the Image of God*, Hereford, Day One Publications, 2004

Croft, L R, *How Life Began*, Darlington, Evangelical Press, 1988

Cuozzo, Dr Jack, *Buried Alive: The Startling Truth about Neanderthal Man*, Arkansas, Master Books, 1998

Garner, C, *Creation and Evolution, Why it Matters what we Believe*, Hereford, Day One Publications, 2008

Gish, Dr D T, *Evolution: the Fossils Still Say No!*, El Cajon, Institute for Creation Research, 1995

Gitt, Dr Werner, *Did God Use Evolution? Observations from a Scientist of Faith*, Bielefeld, Christliche Literature-Verbreitung, 1993

Ham, Ken, *The Lie: Evolution*, Green Forest AR, Master Books, 1987

Ham, Ken, Don Batten and Carl Weiland, *One Blood: The Biblical Answer to Racism*, Green Forest AR, Master Books, 1999

Hanegraaff, Hank, *The Face that Demonstrates the Farce of Evolution*, Nashville TN, Word Publishing, 1998

Haville, M, *Life's Story, the One that Hasn't been Told*, Hereford, Day One Publications, 2004

Heinze, Thomas F, *The Vanishing Proofs of Evolution*, California, Chick Publications, 2005

Johnson, Phillip E, *Darwin on Trial*, Downers Grove MI, Inter-Varsity Press, 1991

———, *Defeating Darwinism by Opening Minds*, Downers Grove MI, Inter-Varsity Press, 1997

Kelly, Douglass F, *Creation and Change*, Fearn, Ross-shire, Christian Focus Publications, 1997

Lebonow, L, *Bones of Contention: A Creationist Assessment of Human Fossils*, Grand Rapids MI, Baker Books, 1992

Morey, Robert A, *The New Atheism & the Erosion of Freedom*, New Jersey, P & R Publishing, 1994

Perloff, James, *Tornado in a Junkyard*, Arlington MA, Refuge Books, 1998

Rosevear, Dr D, *Creation Science, confirming that the Bible is right*, Chichester, New Wine Press, 1991

Sanford, Dr J C, *Genetic Entropy and the Mystery of the Genome*, New York, Elim Publishing, 2005

Sarfati, Dr J, *Refuting Compromise: a Biblical and Scientific Refutation of 'Progressive Creationism' (Billions of Years) as Popularised by Astronomer Hugh Ross*, Green Forest AR, Master Books, 2004

——, *Refuting Evolution: a Response to the National Academy of Sciences Teaching about Evolution and the Nature of Science*, Green Forest AR, Master Books, 1999

Schaeffer, Dr Francis A, *Genesis Space and Time*, London, Hodder & Stoughton, 1973

Spetner, Dr L M, *Not by Chance*, New York, The Judaica Press Inc., 1997

Taylor, Paul, *Truth Lies and Science Education*, Hereford, Day One Publications, 2007

White, Dr A J Monty, *How Old is the Earth?'*, Durham, Evangelical Press, 1991

——, *Wonderfully Made*, Durham, Evangelical Press, 1989

Yumauchi, Edwin, *The Stones and the Scriptures*, London, Inter-Varsity Press, 1973

General: covering a wide range of subjects

Ashton, Dr D (ed.), *In Six Days, Why Fifty Scientists Choose to Believe in Creation*, Sydney, New Holland, 1999

Blanchard, Dr John, *Is God Past His Sell-by Date?*, Darlington, Evangelical Press, 2002

Gish, Dr D T, *Creation Scientists Answer their Critics*, El Cajon, Institute for Creation Research, 1993

Ham, Ken, *How Could a Loving God…?*, Green Forest AR, Master Books, 2007

———, *The New Answers Book*, Green Forest AR, Master Books, 2007

Heinze, Thomas F, *Creation vs. Evolution Handbook*, Grand Rapids MI, Baker Publishing Group, 1988

Lamont, A, *21 Great Scientists Who Believed the Bible*, Acacia Ridge, Qld, Answers in Genesis, 1995

Rosevear, Dr D, *Has Darwin Had His Day? What the Scientific Journals Say*, Portsmouth, Creation Science Movement, 2007

Bible versions

Stern, David H (trans.), *Complete Jewish Bible*, an English version of the *Tanakh* (Old Testament) and *B'rit Hadashah* (New Testament), Clarksville, Jewish New Testament Publications Inc., 1998

Good News Bible, Bible Society, 1976

New International Version (NIV), International Bible Society, 1984

Revised Authorised Version (RAV), Samuel Bagster & Sons Ltd, London, 1982

The Evidence Bible, compiled by Ray Comfort, Orlando, Bridge-Logos, 2003

1315930R0

Printed in Germany
by Amazon Distribution
GmbH, Leipzig